Second Age

Second Age

A Recall of Things Gone By and a Bit of Now

Carl. A. Franson

No part of this book may be reproduced mechanically or electronically, stored in a retrieval system or transmitted by any means, electronic, mechanical, photocopying, recording, or otherwise, without the written permission of the author.

© 2004 by Carl A. Franson, All Rights Reserved.
2nd Printing 2013, Art and Nature, All Rights Reserved

ISBN: 978-0-9855109-4-7 (Paperback, 2013)

Dedicated to my wife
and our children

Second Age

Acknowledging the Author

When my father was in his late 80's, he decided to write about an earlier time in his life during which he experienced and learned much and that profoundly influenced him. He grew excited at the prospect of setting down memories, often he paced to and fro, and he re-lived much of what he recounted here. He remembered sounds, sights, tastes, and smells, and felt almost as if he were experiencing those adventures again, something that surprised, amazed and delighted him. He wanted to share what life and time had relegated to years long since gone by. Some time after he had passed away, it became my privilege to publish this portion of his writing in his memory.

Sonya Franson, daughter

Table of Contents

Introduction 9

Part I

The Floating House 13

Downriver 26

Across Lake Pepin to Wisconsin 41

River Ice Begins 50

Winter in the Shelter of the Wing Dam ... 60

Spring Thaw 70

Farewell to the Floating House 84

Part II

Out to San Francisco 90

The President Coolidge 98

Through the Inland Sea 110

Under the Southern Cross 119

Last Voyages on the President Coolidge 132

A Little about People and Times 138

Index 144

Second Age

Graduation picture of me taken in 1929, from the School of Agriculture at the St. Paul campus of the University of Minnesota. I had completed two years at the college level before becoming entangled in the adventures I relate here.

Introduction

Ancient philosophers, wise in many things, have informed us that there are four ages in a person's life: first, that of childhood; second, that of learning, of testing, and adventure; third, that of service; and fourth, that of the Golden Age.

I am now in my Golden Age writing about a long ago Second Age. To guide me I had a detailed map of the Upper Mississippi and could refer to a published book written by Clarence. Practically all other information has been lost.

Finally getting started, I began to write this letter and was amazed and delighted that scene after scene would be recalled in my mind, sometimes with crystal clear clarity that would also arouse my feelings. I was literally reliving these experiences and one time I became so excited that I had to get up and walk around the room to calm myself and my beating heart.

You will probably notice an absence of specific dates. The timetables have been lost and I do not like them anyway; they are of no value here.

What I have written about covers a period of two years. Most of this time was spent among people of little wealth and making do with what they had. The ship period was among opulence, riches, the best of everything, and famous people. I liked a little of each and strove toward that goal in our Third Age.

You will wonder why I didn't write about girls. Well, I was just so interested in traveling, adventuring, and pursuing my goal that I just did not want any diversions. Sure, the main topics of conversation and the jokes and the ogling was of the opposite sex, and I had desire and opportunity, but I kept "steady as she goes" as a sailor would say. Who is to say that my actions were wise, but for me, I thought I did well.

Now here's my story...

Second Age

Part I

Second Age

The Floating House

In the beginning, there were three of us: Shorty, Clarence, and me, all students in our second year of college at the University of Minnesota at the Saint Paul Campus. In this winter of 1931 we were living in a rented summer cottage on the shore of beautiful Lake Johanna, which was approximately four miles north of Saint Paul. We had two cars; mine was an old model A Ford with a rumble seat.

This enchanting lake was perhaps five miles either way and surrounded by trees to the north, a country road with many cottages to the west, and to the east a Catholic school for emerging priests where, in addition to the handsome buildings and grounds, they had a short, finely crafted wooden bridge connecting to a small island. This small island was heavily wooded, and at the top of its hill and accessible by path only, stood a small but majestic chapel whose melodious bells we could hear at the cottage.

To the west, and across the road, was the Ernest Sanders Farm. Great people---we made arrangements to buy a quart of milk from him each day for ten cents. So each morning, when he was hand milking his cows, we would go over with a dime and a one gallon pail. Many times we would return with almost a full bucket. On one or two occasions we milked his herd for him, so I guess in the end, we all came out even.

A short distance around the lake to the south another rancher named Tony Gauzer lived, and it was through him that we gained a road to the lake shore for our building project.

We three had been together, more or less, through all four years at the School of Agriculture and two years at the college. We had experienced dormitory life together. Then we three, plus five other male students, rented a whole house for three semesters. Our minds were hungry for knowledge, and we would get into long and sometimes heated discussions about many things, but especially about religion. And in some cases these would go on until the wee hours in the morning. Then the next day we would go to the library and get more ammunition for the argument that was sure to occur that night.

For my part, I took to visiting a different church, with a different ritual, every Sunday. The most intellectual church to me was the First Unitarian Church held in the Palace Theater on North Avenue in Minneapolis. Dr. Dietrick was the lecturer. But a church service I have never forgotten was held in an old warehouse. The pulpit was a large barrel on which a kerosene lamp was placed. The pews were just benches without backs, and the roof beams were blacked by coal fires. We sat off to one side on a kind of raised floor. As the poor, mostly colored people arrived, they seemed so depressed and beaten down that our hearts went out to them, but when the minister took over and the singing and praying went on, it seemed as if by magic their cares and woes went away. At the time, I then thought this must be one of the better religions, because it was practicing the law as discovered by our great religious leaders: that love is a greater power than hate.

We had just paid another month's rent, and believe me, money was hard to come by at that time. So we conceived the idea of building a house on the lake to get away from renting. About a week later we made our decision. Our idea was a house on the water, not a houseboat. For this purpose, then, we decided to use fifty-five gallon empty oil drums which were free for the asking at that time. Those would float our house nicely.

About one mile west of the university there was an oil distributor with a huge stack of these empty barrels, and I secured permission to take as many as I wanted. I was able to put one barrel in the rumble seat, then tie one on each front fender of the model A. Three each trip, after school or work on Saturdays. In this manner we moved eighty-eight drums to the lake shore, except on my last trip a motorcycle cop stopped me a mile from our house, and made me unload the two fender mounted barrels. They obstructed my vision, he said, and of course he was right.

Now came the question of lumber. In the early history of Minnesota it was the custom for logging crews to cut the trees in winter and skid them to the nearest navigable waterway or stream and there pile up the logs on the ice (mythology says Paul Bunyan and his blue ox "Babe" did most of the work). In the spring, when the ice melted, the logs floated into the Mississippi River and down to Minneapolis. About one mile north of St. Anthony's Falls (where the huge sawmills were once located), a barrier to catch and hold the logs was built. Every year, however, a few logs would sink to the bottom and stay there. Meanwhile, the supply of logs had dried up, and the large mills closed and were gone when our need for cheap lumber arose. As it so happened, an enterprising father and son team had devised a means of hooking onto these sunken treasures and hauling them ashore to a very small saw, where they put out one board at a time with their own labor. It was from these two that we ordered all of our dimension lumber which they delivered about the time I had our last barrel home.

It was now January, and the ice was thick on the lake. Roy became the chief architect and master carpenter, furnishing the know-how and the tools and skilled labor.

First, we tightened all the plugs in the barrels, then rolled them out onto the ice and lined them up in four rows, all eighty-eight of them. Next, we carried out the long stringers and fitted them over the barrels lengthwise so each twenty-two were held in a slot. Then, crosswise, we nailed planking, and when that was completed, we had a platform. Onto this platform we now built our house, leaving a walkway on each side and rear, plus an open porch in front. We used regular two by four construction for side walls, but for the roof, Roy had cleverly cut the top of two by twelves in a bow shape. When roofed, the rain would run off.

Yet another enterprising man had derived a system to sew twenty thicknesses of newspapers together on both sides. He had gone bankrupt and was selling his stock of newspaper insulation very cheaply. This was used in the ceiling and walls. It was heavy but worked very well. Somehow we acquired enough material to complete the outside, the doors, windows, and enough plywood to build and complete two large chests of drawers and four bunk beds.

This is early construction of our house on the ice of Lake Johanna. All the fifty-five gallon oil drums are in place. The deck, rounded roof rafters and two by four studding are ready.

I kept going to school and working all of this time but still got in a lot of hours building our house on the water. Now it was just a matter of time until we picked up all the different items we needed: a beautiful wood cook stove from the dump out of Anoka, two mattresses from Goodwill, and others.

Here the ice has all melted and we are floating on the lake close to where construction began. We drove posts into the mud to anchor us firmly in place and had a narrow gangplank reaching to the shore. It's very early in spring and the trees are unleafed --- soon we will move on.

It was March, the smell of spring was in the air, a few warm days had occurred, and one late afternoon when I drove into our bay, here was our house floating as proud as a swan on a small ice-free puddle of water. What a sight and what a sensation. We're also sure glad we had thought to put out an anchor rope, because if all the ice had melted, we could have had our house blown anywhere around the lake.

Second Age

Well, all the ice finally did melt, and we pulled the house westward about one hundred yards and anchored it in a bed of cattails or bulrushes, and put down a gangplank to shore. Then we got busy moving from our cottage rental, just in time, as our rent was about due.

Almost immediately we became enthralled with our new lifestyle. At dawn the red wing blackbirds, clinging to the swaying cattails, would sing their hearts out. A large oak tree close by provided perches or nesting places for robins, canaries, a hoot owl, and of course the mournful mourning doves. All of these exercised their voices for our pleasure. Then there were the ducks and geese with nests and the hatching of young close by, the long legged sky pokes and cranes, and then at eventide, the chorus of frogs. We cherished every single minute there.

It's summer time on Lake Johanna. Trees are in full leaf. The birds are all back. And we are truly enjoying our new life while we complete our building.

Now college was over for the summer, and we were working full time. My immediate boss was Dr. Wilson, and he furnished the brains and I the muscle. I was really interested in this project of developing new corn, oats, and barley varieties. After a day in the hot sun, wearing usually nothing but swimming trunks, it was sure pleasant to arrive home and just go to the back of our house and jump into the cool lake.

By now we had built a flat bottom scow or boat, propelled by two oars. It was great sport to row over to the school's island, where they had built a rather large float with three diving boards, one about twenty-five feet high. On a very dark night, and on a dare, I dived off this board into total blackness. Once was enough.

On one occasion we landed on the island and took a path to the chapel. It was about eleven p.m. and the frogs were singing their last rendition for the day. There was a sort of fog in the low places, and spider webs each wore a bit of moisture which was reflected by the partly clouded moon. As we came into the clearing wherein the chapel stood, a single brilliant ray of moonlight enveloped this sacred shrine. We stood in wonderment, then returned to our house, each with his own thoughts.

Thus the summer passed. Tony Gauzer, our farmer friend just south of us, loved to grow a big garden so we had all the veggies we could eat, his compliments.

One day in late summer, a deputy sheriff arrived and served a notice to us to vacate the lake. They had received a complaint and had passed a special law to make the notice legal. We could have purchased a lot and moved to dry land, but having tasted our new life, we did not want to do that. We also could have moved to another lake, but eventually they would move us off that, too. Our solution was to move to a navigable river, namely, the Mississippi.

Having made that decision, we had to find a place to launch, and almost at once found a spot just below the Washington Avenue Bridge on the St. Paul side of the river.

We were also really lucky to find a retired house mover who would take on this task just so he could say he had finally moved his last house. We arranged to let him know where and when to come, and then he would bring out the timbers, jacks, cribbing, etc. Our shore was too muddy, so we had to move the house across the lake where there was a gravelly, sandy beach next to the road. Again our luck held. A south breeze sprang up. We pulled in the gangplank after work that night, untied the house lines, used our pike poles to push free of our wonderful cattail spot and across the lake we went, gently pushed by this slight breeze.

We calculated that we were going to miss our target so tied our rowboat to the front and made most of the correction that we needed by rowing. As we approached shore we used our pike poles to position us into the exact place we wanted to be. It was about three a.m. when we finally arrived, but we had taken turns sleeping so were in pretty good shape.

I went to work at the University that day while Clarence stayed at home to receive the house moving equipment. We were to jack the house up on the cribbing he brought and then move the barrels to the beach. This turned out to be quite a challenge, because the wind had whipped up, and it was difficult to hold the house stationary. Also, we needed to start with some cribbing in the water, but it kept floating away. However, the next day was Sunday, and between the two of us, by hook and by crook we succeeded in raising the house and getting cribbing all in place.

The next day at daylight the mover and a helper arrived with two trucks. One truck was a large flatbed and on it we loaded all of the barrels. The other was an old chain drive Mack truck with solid rubber tires and was equipped with a power winch. In barely readable, formerly gold letters on the rusted doors was the once proud sign "Harris & Son, House Movers". From the back of this towing truck, he unloaded dollies. These had steel wheels with approximately eight inch wide rims. We were in for a nasty ride. By use of the power winch and a crowbar, he very expertly maneuvered the dollies into place under our house, removed the cribbing and lowered the house onto the dollies. After loading the cribbing and jacks, he backed his truck to the front dolly and slipped a clevis pin in place. Checking it all out once more, he said, "Let's go". It was nine a.m. and we were off to a whole mess of unplanned adventures. Our original plan was to live in the house on the river and complete our education, but circumstances intervened, and we never did get back to college.

We were riding in the house and had barely started when we realized we had to practically tie everything down inside. We placed our dishes onto our beds, along with everything we had that was breakable. Our cook stove even started to dance around, and the stove pipe came down in a cloud of black soot. The noise and the vibration from those steel wheels was really something as he pulled us along with two wheels mainly on the rough shoulder of the road, because the house was about fifteen feet wide, and he wanted to leave as much clearance on the road as possible for traffic.

Soon we turned onto Raymond Street, past the University campus, where there was more traffic, and cars were parked on either side making the passing very narrow indeed. I glanced up to see the dormitory, on a small hill to the left, and remembered my first day six years ago when my new life as a student had begun. Then suddenly a dry metal to metal screech emanated from beneath us, so loud, in fact, that the driver stopped at once and came back to find an axle and wheel hub hot. Nothing to do but jack up the axle, remove wheel, and inspect. Thank gosh, although it was badly scarred, he got a bucket of old fashioned axle grease (black and sticky), and gave it a liberal coating. Meanwhile cars were piled up ahead and behind, and honking started and tempers flared. All of this did not bother Mr. Harris at all; he just took his time, and when he was fully ready, jumped into the tow truck and we again began our march.

Como Avenue was a wide and busy thoroughfare with a stoplight. When we came to cross over it and two sets of street car tracks, I thought our house would shake itself to pieces. Soon we were on University Avenue, a wide, smooth street, and rolled along in great shape, but there was more. We now turned to our right onto a short, rough street and crossed over about six sets of railroad tracks. He really did slow down for these or we would have simply disintegrated. We now turned onto Washington Street, going west, and the bridge over the Mississippi River was just ahead, maybe two blocks. Our destination was across this busy avenue, down a short road to a fairly level spot on the river's bank. We proceeded up this avenue, then began our left turn onto this last short road when it happened.

A linchpin in the first dolly had worked loose; the truck moved forward, but the house stayed. We were stuck crosswise across this busy avenue, and that's when the police arrived and confusion reigned supreme. It took Mr. Harris almost an hour to realign the holes and get the linchpin replaced. All this time, the police were handling traffic, including a speeding ambulance, two screaming fire engines, and a funeral convoy. Finally hooked together again we moved off, with great relief, onto our last road, down to our flat spot, where he turned the house around and backed it to the river's edge. It was about four p.m.

but we all just sat there for a while to get our shattered nerves together. Then we jacked up the house, put the cribbing in place, removed the dollies, unloaded the barrels, and we were moved, as far as Mr. Harris was concerned. He would return to pick up the cribbing and the balance of his money in a week. We were sure about the cribbing but not so sure of the money.

Our first task was to put things back in place and clean up the mess, especially the black soot, which was now over everything. We had tied the stove in place, but it had continued to dance and the legs wore scars into the floor that remained through the years.

Our next task was to get the barrels under the house and all back into the water. This sounds simple to do, but it wasn't. We began by digging out an inlet from the river parallel with the back of the house, into which we would place our first row of barrels. The dirt we threw into the river, where the current quickly carried it way. We decided that four barrels only was very little to buoy up the house, so tried to widen for another row, but ran into rock. We had a round, used telephone pole which we planned to use as a roller, and two planks to place on the ground for it to roll on. When the cribbing was removed, then the house would rest at a sloping angle to conform to the sloping land. We carefully removed cribbing and lowered the house onto the four barrels and the round roller. Nothing happened. It just sat there at an angle. We tried using pry poles and even pushed with the car, but nothing worked.

We now dug a hole with great difficulty in the rocky soil on the upper side and put in it a post, against which we placed a jack which did push the house up out into the river, enough for us to place another row of four barrels. The house now sat so low in the water at the back that we could not get the barrels under it, because of their buoyancy. Again began the laborious process of jacking the house up on the river end enough to slip the barrels under their respective slots. Then we'd go to the front and jack the house once more out into the river, enough for another set of barrels. We repeated this process about ten or twelve times, and now one of us had to get into the dirty, filthy, cold water to guide each barrel into place. Finally, with about forty barrels in place, the house slid into the water. As the barrels rolled up in each slot, all of them were at the front end, while there were none at the back, and the house sat low in the water. Also, the river current caught it, and we had to place guy wires up to hold our now floating house in place, in order to install the remaining barrels, after we had turned it around.

Our house mover had put us as close to the Mississippi River as he could. Our job was to get all the barrels under our house and get it all into the water. Simple, right? Wrong.

Our problem now was to submerge each barrel enough to slip into each slot. Each empty barrel would require approximately four hundred pounds downward pressure to fully submerge, so we thought we were needing maybe one hundred fifty to two hundred fifty pounds to partially submerge. We devised a two prong lever system, and working waist deep in water, we forced each barrel into place. Each barrel was easier to install, as the previous one had added to the buoyancy, and soon they were all in place, and we were fully afloat and on a level keel.

There was a small spring of cold water falling from a low cliff to the south of our landing. Under this, we soaked and scraped our bodies of the river filth and really rejoiced that our landing job was now complete, and that this was the last cold shower.

Now came a time of decision. We had had a beautiful summer. We could or would not stay, even though full of work and with not much time or money for play. Both St. Paul and Minneapolis were still discharging raw sewage into the river, and the spot we had unwisely chosen was absolutely putrid. We could or would not stay there longer than necessary. We had been in school for six years and may have lost a bit of our hunger for knowledge, but I think we were really smelling adventure ahead, "keening the wind" as a hunter would say of his dog. We therefore decided to take a year off and go down the river with our floating house. That was a good decision, and now our enthusiasm knew no bounds and we immediately began making plans.

Second Age

Downriver

First we felt that we needed some sort of power to help us maneuver into the many locks and dams on the river and also to get us out of the way of coal barges, etc., that plied the stream. We therefore hunted high and low for a good, used, outboard motor, but with our limited means finally gave up and settled for two Model T Ford engines, complete with transmissions and propeller shafts for five dollars each. By hook and crook we also acquired two propellers (not the same size), and also two forward or reverse thrust bearings. Using scrounged lumber we mounted the engines on the porch, one on each side. Our theory was that when we wanted to turn, we would accelerate one engine in forward and the other in reverse. This would push one side ahead and pull the other one back. (We were definitely not engineers.) After much measuring, trying, and fitting, we were ready for a test, and with both engines running, we slowly backed out into the current and then tried to get back to our landing, but would have failed except for a rope we had left tied to a tree, and our pike poles.

There were several defects in our design. First, with two engines, it required both of us to operate; second, we couldn't see where we were going; third, it didn't control or steer the house worth a damn; fourth, the propellers were too big, or had too much pitch, so we could not accelerate the engines much beyond high idle, so we had very little horsepower to work with.

Well, the time was running into early fall, and if we were going, we had to get, pronto. I had informed Dr. Wilson of our plans, and he was very cooperative and interested, and allowed me to work up to the very last day before our planned departure, on a Sunday. We had spread the word around of our planned departure, to be at twelve noon, and during the last evenings of our stay many friends came by with their well wishes and gifts of one kind or another. It was really exciting.

On the appointed day, our morning was filled with last-minute preparations, but at twelve noon, we, my brother Irving, and Virginia pushed off into the current, and our trip had begun. People on the Washington Bridge cheered and waved us on as we slowly floated without power downstream, and when we passed under the Franklin Avenue Bridge, we were again cheered and waved on.

Our elevation on the river at this point was about six hundred eighty-five feet, so if we ever did reach the mouth, that is the amount we would lose. It was downhill all the way.

We continued to drift with the current and the help of a slight breeze from the north, past Meekers Island, and with densely populated Minneapolis on one side and St. Paul on the other. The river was murkier and filthier, if that was possible. In due time, we spotted the twin cities lock and dam and started our engines to try and head us directly into the chute. Within five minutes, one of the engines blew a head gasket so we shut them both down, then stood ready with our pike poles. Amazingly the current pulled us almost directly into the lock, and after we exchanged a few pleasant words with the operator, he closed his back lock, opened the front one a little way and gently lowered us to the next level. Again, the current took over, and about a mile below the lock and directly across the river from where the famed Minnehaha Creek entered the river, we used our pike poles to push to shore on the St. Paul side,

Second Age

where we tied up for the night. It had not been a dull day. That night we feasted on many of the goodies our friends had brought us, especially those that would not keep without refrigeration.

We still had a number of loose ends to complete so decided to stay where we were for that day, because we could catch a street car close by (we had sold our cars). We therefore tallied our staple food items as follows: a fifty pound sack of dry beans, twenty pounds of sugar, two gallons of molasses, a large, one hundred pound sack of potatoes, a twenty-five pound crate of raisins, a twenty-five pound sack of rice, a twenty-five pound sack of wheat, twenty-five pounds of onions, twenty-five pounds of rolled oats, twenty-five pounds flour, plus sundry baking powder, baking soda, spices, etc. Also, our folks had sent along a home cured ham and two slabs of bacon, real prizes to us.

We also had four, almost-always-in-use utensils, namely, two five-gallon milk cans with covers, the kind in which farmers ship milk or cream to the creamery. One was for fresh water which we carried from sources on shore, and the other was for buttermilk or skim milk, both throwaways at a butter or cheese factory and free to us for the asking. The other utensils were two three-gallon tinned buckets. Almost every small riverside town we were to visit would see us carrying a five-gallon milk can between us and each a bucket in the other hand. Our return saw us with buckets full of fresh vegetables, fruit and groceries, our five-gallon case full of butter, or skim milk, or fresh water.

Monday saw us cleaning up most of the odds and ends, but we returned quite late so decided to stay another night.

We were now ready to begin our southward journey in earnest so untied and pushed off into the faster current. We were still surrounded by a busy St. Paul and could hear traffic on both sides rushing and rushing while we traveled quietly, and slowly we passed the entrance

Downriver

to Pig's Eye Lake, Red Rock, and Newport, and Iver Grove and finally St. Paul's Park, where one mile below, we tied up for our second night. We had traveled a distance of about twelve miles. That's about what our pioneer people did with their oxen on their trek west. It was here that Irving and Virginia left us and caught a bus home.

We pushed off early nest morning, but early on a brisk breeze came up from the south, which was almost strong enough to counteract the power of the river current. We were traveling very slow indeed and late afternoon found us only three and one-half miles downstream. We were guarding our gas supply carefully for an emergency, so did not use power. We tied up at Pine Bend on the inside curve. Frost had already come to the land, and the foliage was in full color. Corn was shocked in neat rows and the pheasants were calling to each other. Already the cares and the worries of our worlds had diminished, and we were becoming receptive to nature and its mysterious beauty.

We were about to sit down for supper when there was the friendly bark of a dog. Clarence went to the door, and this dog immediately bounded aboard and came into our kitchen. At first glance, he appeared to be a German Shepherd, but noting his powerful haunches, I decided he was a neighborhood mix. You know, that doggone dog came right up to me, sat down and held up his paw for me to shake, all the time looking at me with a mischievous, friendly grin-like stare, as if to say: "Hi ya, matey. So we're going on a trip, are we?" Withdrawing his paw, he inspected our bunks both top and bottom on both sides, then went up to Clarence and offered his paw to him. Then he nosed the door open and went out, walked around the outside, came back to the front porch, laid down, and went fast asleep, secure in the knowledge that he had us both hooked good. And we certainly were. He was a fully grown but young dog in perfect health, teeth white and coat shiny. Scraps of food from our table went untouched, and for the six months he was with us, never once did he eat of our food, nor once did we ever see him eat anything. He apparently had his own method of getting anything he wanted for he was always robust and in the best of health. The outstanding thing about him was his personality (almost human) and his endless joy in living.

Next day the wind was still blowing from the south even stronger, so we decided to take our single shot twenty-two rifle, with twenty-two long loads for it, and hunt for a fat gray squirrel, maybe a rabbit or perchance a pheasant. I cruised through the west side of a corn field and entered a small wooded area where I did shoot a nice squirrel out of an oak tree. Bagging him, I started to retrace my steps along this trail when, passing a large bush, here sat our dog, waiting, with that quizzical, half humorous look in his eyes and kind of comical grin on his face as if to say, "Ha ha, we are really having fun, ain't we?" Now he didn't follow me home, because he was his own dog, but he did arrive shortly after.

I dressed out the squirrel and put the carcass to soaking while Clarence finished up some writing he was about. We named our dog Jack.

About noon the wind subsided, so we untied and pushed out into the current. Jack couldn't have been any happier. He stood on the very front edge and alternately stared into the water directly in front of the boat or intently watched the slowly passing shoreline. We traveled about five miles and tied up on the inside curve of the river, on Gray Cloud Island.

The water had now cleared up a whole lot and soon we would start fishing. One group of five barges, loaded with black coal aboard, had moved north, pushed by a puffing sternwheeler. We were informed that each barge held the equivalent of seventy car loads, so here was the same as five seventy-car trains being pushed against the river's current by one small but powerful shallow draft boat, with its dripping rear paddle wheel churning fiercely and flashing in the sun. Another group of six barges moved south. They were empty and riding high in the water, and with the current in their favor they moved quickly past. Because the river was very shallow in places, the boat builders tried to design boats with the least possible draft. The story goes that a contest was held to see who could build a paddle wheeler that would go in the shallowest water. It was won by a boat that would travel on only a heavy dew, but on its test run, the captain got drunk and ran up onto a farmer's corn field, and when the sun came out, the dew evaporated, leaving all stranded.

We were just now beginning to realize what a powerful, magnificent living thing the Mississippi River really was. And we would learn much more as to how it was master of all its domain.

Now the wind had changed to the north, and at dawn we pushed out into the current, moving at a good pace all day and arriving at the Hastings lock and dam at sundown. Again we entered the lock without incident and gently lowered, to be spit out and returned to a much narrower river. One mile further and we tied up at the Hastings city dock. It was dark by then.

We were hoping for mail here, especially my last check from the University. Come morning we carried our two buckets and our five-gallon milk can uptown. Noting first the location of the Post Office, we then found directions to the creamery and there collected our five gallons of fresh buttermilk, no charge. It was a beautiful Indian summer morning, and walking back, we stopped on the sidewalk to chat with a lady who was working in her large vegetable garden beside her home. Maybe we looked hungry, but she was putting the garden to bed for the winter anyway so offered us our choice of anything or everything we might want. We filled both buckets to overflowing with carrots, pars-

Second Age

nips, huge squash, turnips, and finished with apples to fill our pockets. There sure were wonderful people everywhere.

By now it was time for the Post Office to open, so while I guarded our treasures, Clarence mailed our letters, picked up mail for us and arranged to forward whatever might yet come. Jack had stayed home that night for the first time, so with all there we again shoved off to the south.

One engine had suddenly stopped the previous day, so we removed the head, thinking another head gasket was blown. Instead, we discovered a piston with a hole in it, and a major overhaul was now in order. Instead, we decided to ditch that engine and move the other to the center of the porch with some kind of a rudder. Also, we decided to secure a better matched propeller to allow the engine to reach higher revolutions per minute and thus increase horsepower. We were learning a few things, weren't we?

Some three miles below Hastings, the St. Croix River joined and increased our river's size considerably. From now on we would travel with Wisconsin to the east and our own Minnesota to our west.

For some time we had traveled with a small anchor to stop us if need be. Also, our anchor rope, one hundred feet of one-half inch sisal, was tied to the left rear corner, and it was our hope that when used, the anchor drag would turn us toward the west bank. The anchor was light, however, so I tied the now useless head from our engine on in addition. Well, as things sometime happen, a stern wheeler pushing three barges suddenly appeared around a bend. Clarence raced to the anchor and threw it overboard but forgot to let go of the rope. There were two splashes: first the anchor, then Clarence and soon a yell as he came up out of the cold, cold water and swam back to our house. When he was safely again aboard, the pushed barges had already passed and we were standing still but closer to the left bank. In this case, our theory seemed to have worked. All this time Jack had been alertly watching our antics and was now sitting at his usual spot on the porch, and seemed to be laughing and laughing. If this was not true, why was he looking at us instead of watching the water and the shore as was his usual interest?

All the glory of autumn seemed to be in this day as we drifted mile after mile through fall colors. There were all manner of water craft skipping about here and there, rafts, boats, high power speedy runabouts (moonshiner's specials), a few house boats built on flat bottom scows, row boats and kayaks. Sometimes there was nobody on the water and it was then, if we stayed inside and quiet, we could see all manner of wildlife along the shore: deer, a bear once in a while, otters, muskrats, a small herd of apparently wild pigs. There were water fowl of many varieties, by the thousands feeding in the shallows, and we floated right through their ranks as if we were just another stick of wood. When we felt the need to harvest one for dinner, we simply poked the twenty-two rifle through the window and popped off a head. Most of the time we drew the floating carcass to us with the pike pole. Or we could always use our rowboat to retrieve it. This day I felt a certain languor, a laziness or I know not what, but I climbed to the roof and stretched out with my eyes to the sky and just let everything kind of soak in. Geese in "V" after "V" were flying south amid much cackling and changing of leadership. Ducks were sailing in from farmers' grain fields. Pheasants were calling from the corn shocks, crows were gathering and selecting their winter quarters, and there was much argument among them. These sights and sounds added to the balmy soft sunshine of fading summer and led me to a pensive but very satisfying feeling.

The river had been fairly straight and the current rather fast, I thought, and in checking the map we figured we had traveled about nineteen miles when we tied up just south of Diamond Bluff on the Wisconsin side near dark.

It was nice and cozy in our house with the wood kitchen fire burning and beans soaking in tepid water for tomorrow's eats. Clarence was deep in concentration trying to put into words some idea or feeling that was his. He was just like a dog chewing on a bone when he got down to putting together a verse, all concentration and attention.

I decided to go for a walk in the moonlight so quietly left, struck a trail that led north and hiked for some time, maybe a couple of miles, then turned to the upland and was cutting across a field of shocked corn when sitting there, big as life, was Jack. Well, he didn't move, just sat there and barely greeted me. I squatted Indian fashion beside him and looked where he was looking. The harvest dust had now settled out of the air, and the large yellow moon had been replaced by a smaller brilliant gray one, the color of newly forged cast iron, one that was sterner and with less love to give. From the river bottom a hoot owl was hooting at whatever hoot owls hoot at, and then I heard a mother pheasant, from inside the corn shock where she and her chicks had taken refuge for the night, quietly soothe her brood.

These sights, sounds, smells, and sensations caused me to contemplate the great works of the Master of the universe and all His creations, and I would have stayed longer, but it was cold and I was chilly. Saying good night to Jack (he just sat there with no acknowledgment), I returned home with a quick stride but still pondering the strange behavior of Jack. Clarence had thoughtfully hung our kerosene lantern up to brighten the narrow gang plank, and I brought it with me into the house and set it on the table. I was removing my shoes and enjoying the warm, cozy feeling of our home when the teakettle sang its last cheerful notes. In that instant I solved the strange behavior of Jack. I remembered the hen pheasant's soothing voice. I had walked up on Jack just as he had found his dinner. He was even now probably dining on young, tender, moist, mostly grown pheasant chick a la corn shock. I went to bed with pleasant thoughts and a certain reverence for the way things are in nature.

It was an hour before dawn, when night was at its blackest, when I became instantly awake, fully alive, alert and completely poised for "fight or flight". Right outside my porthole a red light about ten feet above the water and ten feet away was slowly passing. This could only be a barge, and yelling like a demon I awoke Clarence and we dashed for the door and out onto the porch. Had this barge come our way just a few feet more, we would have been reduced to kindling wood, blood and bones, and the river would have moved on coughing up the debris. Then there would have been a little talk of he and me, then no more talk of me or he.

Standing on the porch in our long underwear in the night's chill, we watched our threat move on. We could hear the throbbing exhaust of the steam engine and the paddle wheel pushing water to the rear. A powerful search light was probing the two shore lines for navigation markers, and all at once it landed on us for a second or two, then whisked away. There were five huge scows in this group, all pushed by one little stern paddle wheeler boat.

It was too late to return to bed, so we poked up the fire, dressed and set the coffee out. We were both elated to learn that our bodies still possessed that intuition that enabled us to become instantly prepared to meet the situation and handle it.

That day we pushed off at daybreak and entered country which seemed full of sloughs. Quaking aspen and willows grew everywhere, and among them muskrats had built thousands of homes. Cattails, reeds

Second Age

and rushes were in profusion, and along a few creeks we spied beaver dams near where young trees had been felled by them. Coming around a bend, there was a farm set back on a piece of higher ground and we heard a dog bark. Jack heard this too, and the next thing we knew he jumped into the water and swam to the shore, where we last saw him climbing a low bank. We were drifting almost out of sight when we heard a dog challenge and then a dog fight begin. We continued to move south while we discussed whether to go to shore and tie up, or to drop the anchor, or to go on. We decided to float onward because we knew that Jack was his own dog, and that he was going to do what he was going to do regardless of what we did. It was late in the afternoon when we heard his bark, and there he was some fifty feet away swimming strongly to us. We grabbed his fur on the back of his neck and gave him just a little help, and that was all he needed to scramble aboard, where he thanked us at once with a cold shower. He then sat down facing us, with that so much like him, quizzical, merry eyes and smiling face as if to say, "Boy, oh boy, was that fun".

We continued onward and tied up that night where farms occupied most of the space. As usual Jack went ashore at once. Morning brought with it a stiff breeze from the south and traveling against it would be impractical. Inasmuch as we were shore bound, we decided to remove the wrecked engine and move the other to the center of the front porch. We had no clear idea how we would do this but knew we needed to scavenge something somewhere, so left our house by itself and took off along one of the many game trails. This river had many islands, and many people, at one time or another, had lived on one or along the shore. Eventually a dim path led us to what we figured was an abandoned still. We spied a small coil of one-half inch copper tubing and a spool of one-eighth inch flexible cable, very rusty, also an old sign of rather heavy sheet metal. These might all be useful, so we appropriated them and returned with our loot. This now stimulated us to plan a regular pilot house on the stern roof and run all the controls from there, using our flexible cable. We would then be traveling backward at all times when using the engine, and this was okay, except to Jack, who loved to stand on the front porch and watch. Finding lumber was no problem as there were many abandoned houses on stilts, or tree houses. While moving the second engine to the middle, Clarence dropped our only hammer into the water. It was of his doing, so he stepped down and went into the icy water to retrieve it. The water was deep and he was barely able to touch the mud below with his feet to feel around to find the hammer. He eventually did, however, and then reversed himself with his feet up and his hands down but could not readily find it so came up for air, dived twice more and finally came up with it. He was blue with cold by then, but the air was warm, the soup hot, and he recovered okay. He learned the moral: "Don't drop your tools in the water."

We expected to be in Red Wing, Minnesota before too long so spent the balance of that day writing letters and doing some needed housework. At dinner, which was of buttermilk and rice soup with raisin pudding, we got to thinking how good fresh, whole milk would taste. Now came an escapade. There was a fairly large and prosperous farm about one half mile back from us, and it looked as if it was a dairy farm, where, in cold weather, they kept the cows tied in stalls. We waited until about two a.m., then each of us, with a bucket covered with dark cloth so the shiny metal would not reflect the moonlight, walked stealthily forward. Jack, who had probably seen our furtive skulking, quietly joined us from somewhere out in the dark. As we approached the barn through the pale moonlight, the farmer's dog suddenly sounded a warning which Jack immediately dashed ahead and answered. In the minutes of the first dog engagement we entered the barn, and finding the cows with the help of a weak flashlight, we kicked up a couple and milked furiously. With about a gallon each and the buckets again covered with our dark cloths we cautiously left the barn again by the same back door and lost no time hurrying home. We could hear Jack and the farmer's dog somewhere down the road on the other side of the house.

It wasn't right what we did, but we enjoyed the fresh milk for several days, and we wondered several times what the farmer thought when he milked the next morning to find two cows not putting out as much milk as usual. It was an escapade not to be forgotten.

We now had the engine moved over to the center of the porch and a makeshift wobbly rudder in place. We pushed off into a rather coolish dark gray day and tried our engine. It worked better that the two engines as far as steering was concerned, but the low RPM, because of the too-large propeller, was the problem. We arrived at Red Wing and tied up on the Wisconsin side just below the bridge about the time when most rural folks were having supper. We had ours, and then taking our kerosene lantern, we picked up a game trail to reach the bridge to cross over into Red Wing. All at once a voice came out of the darkness. "What the hell are you doing here? Get out!" to which we replied, "We just came in on our floating house and need to go uptown." He said, "You can't make it up this boulevard without a drink, come in."

Well, he had a shanty a few feet farther on, almost hidden in the shrubbery, a dirty lantern was on the table with hardly any light coming through the smoke blacked chimney, and a gallon jug of moonshine half empty beside it. We sure did not want to be his guests but felt the need to be neighborly. He tilted the jug to his lips for a good swig, then passed to us where we each did likewise, except used our tongue to stop the flow. Much of the moonshine at that time was flavored with anise seed and this sample must have had a heavy dose, for it seemed I tasted it for most of two days. After another round and much babble we left with good directions to get to the road, and a much easier and better way to return to our house.

This town was the home of the famous Red Wing Shoe Company, maker of fine leather sport and hunting boots We walked past this, located the Post Office, and the creamery and an iron foundry, where we noted a large grinding wheel, which gave us the idea of cutting the size of our propeller down. Rising early we were at the creamery around seven a.m. and secured our buttermilk, no charge, and carried it back to the house. Returning at once, while Clarence went to the Post Office, I took our spare propeller to the foundry to see if it could be ground down. When I asked my question of a man who looked like he might be a foreman, he looked at me closely and asked, "Were you and another boy carrying a milk can over the bridge this morning?" "Yes," I said. Anyway, after more visiting, he took the propeller and expertly ground about one third off the back of each blade and balanced it as well as he could. Handing it to me he said no charge and good luck.

News from home and friends at the University was good for me, while Clarence received a check for some poetry he had submitted. We were feeling great with a few bucks in the pot again.

It took just a few minutes to replace the propeller with the modified one and being egged on by an impatient Jack, we pushed off. About five miles downstream, we came to a slow gradual, and then complete, stop. We were stuck on a sandbar. Our best efforts to push together on our pike poles, back or forth, sideways or one end at a time, all went unrewarded, We finally rowed to shore with our flat boat and secured two stout pry poles, but these were also inadequate, so we just sat there and wondered what to do next. Late in the day, a stern wheeler, pushing four

Second Age

loaded scows, went by and believe me we were ready with our poles. When the backwash came in, we pushed furiously and with success. Another one half mile and we entered Lake Pepin headwaters.

Across Lake Pepin and On Downriver

Lake Pepin is a large, long, deep body of water with the Mississippi running in one end and out the other. Its destiny was to be one of the great water sports resort areas of the Midwest. It seemed to have everything, both summer and winter.

We traveled somewhat east by south as the deep channel was close to the west shore, where the heavy traffic would be. At dark we pushed into the shore and tied up. There was hardly any current in the river, and this was the first time this had happened since leaving Lake Johanna; it seemed months ago. It was not quite dark, so I went ashore to rustle up some stove wood if possible, while Clarence lit the lamps and prepared dinner. We had quite naturally assumed our everyday work. I liked to hunt game and rustle up wood while Clarence liked to cook (and he was quite good at it). Other tasks like washing clothes and cleaning floors we more or less did together. I also liked to fish, and now, with clean cold water under us, I opened the trap door under the table and dangled a line, with several hooks attached, among the floating barrels. I tied the line to a piece of bicycle tire inner tubing, closed the door and replaced the table. I would check this line twice a day to remove fish, if any, and re-bait the hooks. We caught mostly sunfish weighing one-half to three-fourths of a pound this way. There were two nice fillets on each, and four made a nice meal for two. This sure was not sport fishing.

Our goal now was to cross over to the Minnesota side and tie up at Lake City about one-half the way down the lake. The south wind had switched to the north, and this was ideal to propel us ever southward with a very sluggish river current. We now started our engine to move us across the lake with our new, modified propeller. Man-o-man, did it ever work great, with the engine now turning up its RPMs and the horsepower pouring down the drive shaft to the propeller. However, when we applied the rudder, it dang near flew apart from the pressure, so we had to cut the engine's RPM. All in all, it was the best performance we had.

We were floating along now close to the western shore when we herd a splash and Jack was gone from his usual spot. Well, we looked and we called, and we looked, but we could see him nowhere. He had just simply disappeared. At least a half hour went by when we heard his bark on the starboard side, and in a moment he was aboard with our slight help, gave us his shower, then sat facing us with that "guess I fooled you guys" look. We finally figured out that he had gone under the boat, come up among the barrels and simply swam along until he found his way out from under.

It was almost dark when we poled into the Lake City harbor of refuge and tied up to our first honest-to-goodness dock, with a plank walkway leading to the street. We had become somewhat celebrities by this time and many people drove by or walked to the street to see the two boys floating a house down the mighty Mississippi, as was reported in the river news bulletin. Other people in past times had gone down in odd ways: an elderly lady had rowed an eight foot rowboat almost to the mouth; another person had paddled an Alaskan kayak; a young man had ridden a log; another floated a bathtub.

By now we began to realize that we were not going to make it down before freeze-up and that our cook stove would not be enough heat to keep us warm. We therefore set out for the town junkyard about a mile out of town and found an old coal burning stove in good condition, but the entire bottom was burned out. We found a short pole and with a light rope we had with us, we tied this on, and with the stove between us, we carried it through town and to our house. We had two sheets of corrugated iron roofing lashed to the roof, and cutting this to size, we placed it on the floor and the stove on top. From lumber we also had on hand, we then built a box eight inches deep, then filled it with bucket after bucket of sand until the missing bottom of the stove became a bottom of sand. It was then simple to install new stovepipe and haywire it through one pane of our window. It looked like heck and stuck out like a sore thumb, but it did the job and was affordable. We also loaded up with a can of free buttermilk, shopped for needed odds and ends, reinforced our wobbly propeller and were now ready to again travel.

Jack did not like towns, and he was restless and eager to get going. However, a strong south wind was blowing and without a strong tide to counteract it, it was impractical to try. Therefore another day passed without progress, but we caught up on a lot of things and really enjoyed the heat from our new stove.

It was the first of November. We arose in the dark at six thirty and noticed a brisk northwest wind blowing, but as that was what we had been waiting for, and since the waves still seemed small and without caps showing, we lost no time in loosening our house's ropes from the dock and starting our engine. Soon we were out past the safety and security of the rock wall and committed to our struggle with the lake. Our idea was to push our house far enough east into the lake so as to pick up some of the river's current, which would assist us from being blown ashore on the south side.

Second Age

The wind kept rising by the minute and the waves became more monstrous and threatening. The engine became useless as a means to direct our path, and as we reached the long sweep of the lake, the wind and the waves just took over and gave us a real good thrashing. Most of the time our house was broadside to the wind and therefore in every wallow and on top of every wave crest. It rocked, careened, went this way and that, groaned, shrieked, rose and fell until we were hard put to it to just hang on. The pictures came off the walls, the books off the shelves, the clock off the desk, the guns rattled to the floor, the waves came over the deck, water through the planking. At times, we came out of our sideways roll, and it was then when one corner of our house was in a wallow, and the diagonal corner was on a crest, that this corkscrew power threatened to pull every spike and nail loose. From the groaning and the screeching we heard, we imagined that this might happen and to the roofing it did, because we had to repair many cracks.

In spite of this ordeal we "rode her out", so to speak, in a happy-go-lucky manner, and our elation and adventurous spirits were high, but not more than Jack, who literally quivered with excitement.

Then the wind lessened, the waves shrunk down, the river's current took charge, and soon we were at the lake's south end and about to enter the river proper. At this point, there were literally thousands upon thousands of waterfowl of all types and kinds. They barely moved out of the way as we drifted among and through them.

Somewhere beyond where the Chippewa River came in from Wisconsin, there was a jog in the Mississippi where a bit of high land stuck out and which looked quite heavily wooded. Our wood box was full, but our extra supply had washed overboard during our wild ride on Lake Pepin. We therefore tied up early and then went hunting for some. We found a dead red oak, probably killed by lightening. It was down and dry, and we soon had two good loads slung over our backs by ropes and two more ready for our next trip.

Having more daylight to use, we took a walk along a heavily used game trail through this elevated area of maybe twenty or thirty acres, and as we approached the other side we heard music filtering to us through the half-leaved trees. A few more steps brought us to where we looked down into a sort of cove in which floated a real houseboat. It was probably four times larger than ours and half double decked. Its hull was flat bottomed, and a heavy-duty gasoline-powered boat was cabled to the rear and used as a pusher, while to the front a separate float carried what looked like a small garden for growing vegetables. We later learned that is exactly what it was. The classical music continued to emanate from the open windows and we moved a bit closer to better hear. At a point, the music stopped, and a man came out and beckoned us aboard.

"Are you the two boys floating a house down the river?" he asked. "Yes," we said. "I thought I recognized you from when I was in Lake City with the boat, filling up with gas," he said.

Their home was beautifully done with a mixture of the sea and the riverboat gamblers motif. Brass lamps and ship's bells decorated the mahogany and teak walls and a polished winding stairs led to their bedrooms above, where there was a small pilot's table before a window looking forward, in the main or master bedroom. It was from this point that they guided their three piece outfit to where they wished to go.

We had been introduced to this man's family when we first came aboard: a middle-age wife, one daughter, perhaps twelve, two boys, one about sixteen and the other maybe eight, and we had learned they were all musicians. A piano, three violins, a viola, and a cello were laying around in one corner where they had just been playing them. As our conversation developed and expanded, we learned that they had spent most of the summer on the beautiful St. Croix River near the town of Stillwater, Minnesota and had performed several times in Minneapolis and St. Paul. They had also performed at the Minnesota State Penitentiary in Stillwater, and of interest too, at the Chippewa Indian Reservation in Wisconsin, where most of the people still lived in their teepees.

On the following morning, they were on their way south and would winter on a small river somewhere in the south, a spot they knew well but I cannot now remember. They were all hooked up so all they had to do was pull in the gang plank, untie, and take off. They would travel at half speed, for economy, and down river at about ten to twelve miles per hour. They were well equipped with powerful search lights, detailed river maps and a confidence of long experience. Usually they would travel one hundred twenty-five miles per day or more if they needed.

For us this was a wonderful experience, to meet such refined and talented people on the river. They had chosen this lifestyle and were living in perfect harmony with their surroundings. Most other people we met were survivors like us, making do with what we had, and that wasn't much. Perhaps, in the long point of view, it was just as well that we did not have adequate finances during our young, restless lives because it "tempered our steel", so to say. However, it made us very sad to see so many people in their Golden Age living hand to mouth in hovels and in poverty, some killing their sensibilities with rot gut moonshine, others in a dream world where only their physical body functioned. It seemed that most of them were soldiers of one kind or another who could never seem to find their way back into society after the battles or training. Most were proud, however, and carried their pride with a sort of belligerence. They would share almost anything they had and would trade with pleasure, but if you tried to give them something they would

Across Lake Pepin and On Downriver

instantly become suspicious, and so we learned lesson after lesson.

We left in the early morning hours while a cold moon was ruling the sky, quickly passed our land outcrop that had given us the nice wood, and passed the cove which our musical friends had left empty. The river had been pushed together by bluffs on both sides, so it was quite straight and the current fast. A pontoon bridge jutted out from both sides, but the center was open, and we jetted through maybe five or six miles per hour. We made a detailed examination of our house structure and pounded in a few nails and spikes that had pulled loose, but in general all was in good condition, despite our Lake Pepin pounding. That is, all except the rolled-type roofing which was cracked and torn. We would have to re-tar and repair it as soon as we could get the material. Oh, yes, we noted one barrel was missing, and maybe more, but we still rode high in the water and did not worry.

It was almost dark when we started our engine and slowly pushed into the inner curve of the river, and tied up beside a grove of swamp alder trees. Jack, as was his wont, immediately dashed ashore and was gone for the night. Clarence had put a pot of beans to soak the previous night, and they were now in the oven approaching their ultimate tenderness and flavor. Checking our map, we figured we had traveled thirty to thirty-five miles, our best yet, and were cheered.

We awoke early and were ready to push off when Jack bounded board, all energy, all happiness, all pleasure and just glad to be with us and looking forward to another day of adventure. We often wondered just what his thoughts were, what he did at night, where he got his food and how. Whatever he did was right, for he was always in perfect condition, and his joy in living knew no bounds.

Our goal now was Winona, Minnesota, where we expected to receive mail, perhaps money, and newspapers with news from home.

Second Age

The mornings now found frost on the earth, and now and then we detected ice on quiet waters. Time was running out for us. Under rather dark and troubled skies, we reached our goal about one p.m., where a small check was waiting for Clarence for some poem he had submitted. Part of this was used to purchase repair material for the roof, and a few necessary groceries. We also collected five gallons of buttermilk and five gallons of skim milk, compliments of the management. It was cold enough so that both would keep until consumed. It was fairly warm that afternoon so we preheated the tar for the roof and then covered every crack we could find in the roofing with flat spatulas that we cut out of some sheet metal we had aboard. We must have done a good job, because nary a leak developed.

It was late in the day, so we decided to lay over, went up town, looked in windows, ogled the girls, visited with a few shopkeepers and returned to our floating house.

Under dark and troubled skies we moved ever southward that Saturday through what must have been an unstable river bed, for there were many rock wing dams in place to keep the river where it now was, and to keep it deep enough for the heavy traffic.

At about four p.m. we tied up at the small town of Trempealeau, Wisconsin, at their dinky dock, and walked up their stairs to the town's level. Having walked through the town, we turned back and noticed a new beer joint (Franklin D. had recently announced, "You shall have your beer"), and stepped in to inquire if they would like some accordion music to dance by. Yes, they would. So after eating our dinner, we carried my accordion there at about eight thirty p.m. Now when you are plain sober, my music was not much, but after a few beers, a polka beat or a waltz rhythm, the happy feet took over from the brain. And nobody noticed whether a note was early, late, or entirely missing. It was fun, and though the crowd was small and times really tough, we still came home with a few dollars for the kitty. We returned home at the river's edge through a sleet of icy snow, and had to sit down on the icy steps one by one, and finally slide down with my music box. We now revived our banked fire and waited for its welcome warmth. The sleet seemed to be coming at us with increasing fury, and we were uneasy because we had tied up on the out curve of the river where the current was fastest and the wind could really get at us.

Second Age

River Ice Begins

The temperature was going down, so we decided to keep the fire going and take turns keeping watch. At about six a.m. we heard a scratching noise on the river's side. We thought at first that it might be rats come aboard. Jack was on the porch and started to scratch on the door, so we got our one flashlight and went out to look. It was then that we saw ice building on the shore and thin ice forming on the river, then breaking up. It was thin ice scraping along the edges of the barrels that had caused the scratching.

I can tell you right now it was bitter, bitter cold with a stiff wind to drive its lesson to the bone, and we re-entered our warm, wood toasted sanctuary, while Jack stayed where he was on the porch. He was telling us that he was better adapted to this environment than we were.

We now had a real problem to face. One way or another, we had to move out of that exposed, dangerous place and somehow find a safer one, or abandon it altogether. While we pondered that, we cooked a hot oatmeal breakfast, with raisins, made some stove lid biscuits, and with this body fuel consumed, now faced the day.

We decided to move. At around eight a.m. while the day before it had been quite light, today was almost as dark as midnight. Having hunted up and changed into all of the warmest clothes that we owned, we now ventured outside and untied the front lower rope, then the rear. Almost at once, the current broke us away from the shore ice, and away

River Ice Begins

we went. We were just another iceberg floating among the many cakes. It was quiet now, and the scratching noise had ceased, because we were floating along at the same speed.

We could have really enjoyed this, except it was so dark we could barely see the shoreline. The bitter cold was building the ice floes, thicker and bigger, and with time would suck the last BTU from the water, and its top would then be one solid sheet of ice. Where would we be when this happened?

Along about noon we felt a slight jar and then noticed the ice floes moving past, at least most of them. Something had hold of us on the bottom, and we didn't know what. Many days later a riverman told us that we had probably caught onto a piling. When such cold grips a river, its many creeks, water falls, and smaller feeder streams freeze up and failure to yield gallonage causes the Mississippi to fall in its level.

Our decks and outwalks were covered with the sleety ice, so we removed ashes from our cook stove and spread them around the porch and catwalks, and also borrowed some sand from our sandbox. We were crosswise with the river, and the ice would build up against us, so we drove spikes into the ends of our pike poles and used them to push the floes to either side. We were afraid the side pressure would build up so great it would break us in half. It was bitter cold, so we could only stay at this for only a few minutes each time, and then we would have to move to the stove to soak up some heat. Also, the slippery footing forced us to hang onto the railing with one hand while pushing ice away with the other. One slip would probably be the last bath we would ever take; at least we thought this.

We then conceived the idea of pushing the ice away from the porch end only, thinking we were hung up on something under the center of the house, and that with ice pressure on one end and none on the other, it would pivot us around and maybe get us free from the demon that clutched us from below. No luck. We simply stayed put. Hovering over the stove, thawing our frozen hands for the tenth time, we now came up with a plan to push the ice floes under the house instead of around the ends. This we did, and while we were again thawing out, there was a slight tremor, and we were free and again just another thing floating helplessly downstream. Somehow we were elated. Now Lady Luck could go to work.

Our situation at about one p,m. was this. The day was still so dark we could barely see the shoreline and its shore ice frozen solid to the shore. The temperature was bitter cold and a sleet laden wind was blowing in from the north. It pushed us a bit faster than the ice floes, which in turn caused our house to turn slowly one way, then another. The ice by this time had grown from wafer thickness to at least two inches. At this point we decided to start our engine and try to maneuver to the Minnesota shore. It took all the hot water we had to get the engine started, and we started to push shoreward, but within three minutes something gave way, either the propeller or the drive line, and we were now without power. We were perhaps seven hundred fifty feet from the Wisconsin shore and decided to use our pike poles against the floes and work our way shoreward. This idea worked surprisingly well, and by working one at a time while the other fed the stove and warmed up we gradually reached the shore ice. But where was a haven, and how could we stop?

We had a one hundred foot coil of one-half inch manila rope on board, and one end of this we tied to the rear shoreward side of our house. We were gong to keep our eyes peeled shoreward to try and find a tree large enough to hold us. I would keep the house as close as possible to the shore ice, and Clarence would jump onto the shore with the

River Ice Begins

rope, wrap it around the tree, and presto! We would be stopped and soon frozen into place.

What actually happened was this. A suitable tree did finally appear through the gloomy dusk. Clarence did leap ashore with the rope but in doing so fell through the shore ice and soaked both feet but good. Scrambling madly over icy shore rocks, he slipped and fell down twice, finally reached the tree and got one wrap around it before the house pulled it taut, and we went on downstream while a wet, uncomfortable, thoroughly beaten boy stood there disgusted. Because of the slippery shoreline he could not keep up with us to come back aboard and was steadily losing distance. At this point, I jumped into the dinghy and rowed against the ice floes and current until he came up and got into the boat, but not without again breaking the shore ice and re-wetting his icy feet. It took some time to regain our house, having to push the floes aside, but we did, and I suppose there was nobody in the world who welcomed the warm stove more than we did.

We now decided to fight no more, to let destiny take its course. We did not even retrieve our now trailing rope. Instead we prepared a good hot meal, now and then peering out into the total blackness and gave ourselves up to the whim of the gods. It had not been a quiet day.

Taking turns sleeping, we noticed the wind going down and the noise of the sleet lessen, and around three a.m. the total darkness seemed to brighten a bit. I guess we both dropped off to sleep, but when morning came and we awoke, we were stopped about two hundred feet below a rock wing dam. The sun was shining, the temperature had risen, and we were locked into a solid sheet of ice. Days later we wondered about just how it was that we got there, because usually the current speeds up on the downstream side of the dam, and most objects are thus pushed toward the center of the river. In our case, it was just the opposite. Then

Second Age

we remembered our trailing rope. It must have entangled itself somehow in the rocks and held long enough to swing us behind the wing dam and into shallow water.

Jack, who had borne this past day with a certain amount of disdain, was ashore when we came out on the porch, and we would not see him again, until tomorrow.

Once again, our spirits soared. If we could survive yesterday, then today was duck soup. There were two immediate problems: first, to move closer to the wing dam and shore, and second, to restock our wood pile, now dangerously low. The ice that held us tightly was about three inches thick. We used our one man crosscut saw and easily and quickly cut ourselves loose, then cut a channel a bit wider than our house, pushed the cut ice under and into the slight current, then pulled the house up this channel until we finally reached the full shelter of the wing dam and within gangplank reach of the shore.

Searching for dry wood was something else, but we finally found a tumbled down shack or shed that had not been used for years, so quickly chopped and sawed it into transportable pieces, and tying on a short rope we had with us, we skidded it to our temporary home, where we reduced it to stove length pieces, filled our wood box and stacked the balance on the porch. Yes, life was good.

We now needed to orient ourselves, to know exactly where we were. We were in a reasonably safe spot, below this high rock wing dam attached to Minnesota Island on the Wisconsin side. Directly across the river there was first a set of railroad tracks and then a well-used highway. A house with smoke coming from its chimney stood alone by the highway, and directly below, by the railroad tracks, there was a water tower used to refill the coal-fired steam engines, and a building housing a telegraph office. It would sure be nice to be over there on the Minnesota side instead of where we were. We were approximately five miles north of La Crosse, Wisconsin, and Clarence decided to hike in there to pick up mail and get a few light supplies as well.

It was a crisp, sunny day, and I decided to explore our lucky island and inventory what we might have to work with during our enforced stay. I would have liked Jack's company, but this was not his way, and though I saw his tracks many times and he came into my path on two occasions, I still went alone. I knew he had me in his scent, hearing and sight at all times. What a remarkable dog he really was.

We both returned to our house before dark and discussed what next to do. It would be a long, tough winter at its best, and we longed to be across the river about a mile or so down and south of a large wing dam we could see there.

However, the river was not done with us yet. A warm breeze had come up from the south and warmed or rotted the ice, and soon all the ice that was in the main channel was moving that night. We were tired so we went to sleep. Well, the ice jammed at the La Crosse bridge, the river must have risen at least ten feet, the house was pushed ashore, the ice dam broke, and the river went down. When we awoke, we were half in, half out of the water at a slant of perhaps thirty degrees. Now our fairly comfortable house was almost useless except as a shelter. We could not use the cook stove or oven, because, due to the excessive slant, they would not hold the pots and pans, so we found some rocks and a dry spot on shore to build a cooking fire Indian style. Our heating stove could still be used, and we kept things warm there by placing vessels beside the stove in the sand.

Now the problem was: how are we going to get back in the water. We needed to move at least eight feet. There were no craft of any kind on the river, and it was still full of icy floes. There was no way we could pull or push sideways to wiggle it down. Our only solution was to jack, pry or push from the porch end.

The propeller was hanging in the air with one very badly bent blade, and we said we must replace it with our spare before final entry into the water. By chance we noticed some water near the engine and found both the head and block badly cracked from freezing up. It was then we remembered that we had overlooked draining when we stopped it during our very bad storm. In disgust, we removed the whole power plant, plus all the spare parts, our fifty-five gallon drum of gasoline with perhaps ten gallons left, cut our wooden mounting into firewood, and we now looked like we originally did when we floated on Lake Johanna so long ago, it seemed.

There was some space under the barrels, so we decided to cut some heavy pry bars about twelve feet long, then jack them up with a heavy screw type truck jack we had. This we did but could not raise the ends high enough to secure a good raise, push and pry action. We had a small hand winch used to raise our rowboat onto davits. This we removed and mounted on the roof, then tied a rope to the ends of the two pry bars, and leading it back to the winch, wound it around the other round bar. Now while one of us turned the crank, the other tightened the rope around the revolving bar, and soon we were exerting considerable pressure in the pry bars, and they were rising upward and pushing mightily. But then there was a crack, and one bar snapped in half. On inspection, we had not moved one single inch.

Late in the day now, we retired to our sloping house, added fuel to the heater, switched our beds from head to foot so we could lie down with our head raised, and prepared for the night. I was not hungry, in fact did not feel quite well, so ate a small cup of hot soup and went to bed, where sometime during the night I developed a high fever with accompanying chills. Aspirin was the only thing we had on board in the way of medication. Morning came, and Clarence said I was out of it mentally and burning up. It scared him half to death, but there was no way he could secure help. Along late that afternoon the fever broke, and I fell into a deep sleep, awakening the next morning feeling rested but weak. I stayed inside and warm all day, while Clarence cooked up a mess of food on the campfire. Now we could just warm it up on the sand by the heater as needed.

No solution to our problem surfaced. That really bad storm had dumped a lot of snow over northern Minnesota. The warm breeze from the south had melted the ice and now the river was running almost ice free. Then a Chinook settled in melting the snow and soon creeks, small rivers, and waterfalls were pouring into the Mississippi, and we gleefully watched the thirty degree slope become twenty degrees, then ten degrees, and we were ready with our pike poles to push off the bank and again become level. What a relief.

By now we knew we could not stay where we were over winter. The next morning was bright and clear, with a warm wind from the south blowing briskly. It was move now or never, and with power it would have been so easy. We attached our rowboat to the house with a rope, and I would row while Clarence would use the pike pole wherever he could. Our first goal was to cross the river and reach the upriver side of the wing dam, before the current bore us downstream. Pushing off, we moved into the channel, where the water was too deep for the pike pole, and where the current was the fastest. Here I really leaned into the oars and thought for awhile we would lose, but that south breeze really helped, and soon Clarence was finding bottom and pushing hard. We came onto the Minnesota shore about a block north of the wing dam. It was then a simple matter to tie up, look the situation over, and devise a strategy to reach our second and final goal: how to maneuver our house into the large pool below this wing dam.

Our plan was to pole along the upper face of the dam until the current grew stronger. Clarence would then climb onto the dam with a one hundred foot rope, and I would get back into the rowboat. The map indicated that the main channel was some three hundred feet beyond the end of the dam, so we could expect not quite as fast a current. Our friendly south breeze was still with us as Clarence climbed the north wall, playing out rope as he went. I slowly began to row, the current took hold, and soon we were at the end of the dam and going around, picking up speed. The dam was higher than it looked and the rope shorter than it needed to be, so no help there. I headed our rowboat toward shore and this time leaned into the oars with everything I had. There was a snap and I fell backwards off the seat. One oar had broken in half. I fished this half out of the water, then pulled myself along the tow rope and reached our house, now again at the complete mercy of the gods and floating helplessly downriver.

Then a miracle happened.

Jack, the house, and I were headed downstream without any means whatsoever to help ourselves, while Clarence watched from the top of the wing dam. Slowly I realized we were not going with the current anymore but were slowly moving toward the shore, and then, of all things, we were moving north and into the very spot we wanted. Soon we were there, and with a bit of pike poling, moved to the shore and stopped. Out went our anchors fore and aft. Then our three-eighths inch high strength cable from a main beam was taken ashore and tied to a stout tree on the bank, about eight feet above us. We were now so cautious that we even wired the hook to the cable, so it could not possibly come loose. Also, that very afternoon we secured two poles and two posts. The posts we set deep into the ground, front and rear. Then we haywired the poles to them and the other ends to the house. This way a wind could not possibly blow us up on the bank again. Now, having the gangplank firmly in place, we called it a good day and retired to our snug cabin, at peace with the world and ourselves, and secure in the knowledge that we were now close to other people and could live with some degree of comfort for a long winter. All in all it was not a dull day.

Regarding this miracle, I later learned from Mr. Daley (whom I will introduce in a page or two) that he had observed the river forming a giant whirlpool, and that he had watched us as we were sucked into the outer rim and were so kindly and gently conducted to our winter's quarters. He had observed the phenomenon several times and said it usually lasted about two hours, and was caused by a certain river level, when water was diverted into a side channel.

The next day was still bright and balmy, but we were still a bit nervous of holding our house steady, so we filled a couple of heavy jute bags with rocks and tied ropes to them, then carrying them in our rowboat, we dropped them to the river side about twenty yards out. Now we had four anchors out, plus a cable to the tree, plus two stout poles holding us steady out and in. It was enough.

Second Age

Winter in the Shelter of the Wing Dam

Again it was time to take stock of our surroundings. The wing dam above us came off a low hill and looked to be at least ten feet higher and twice as long as the first one we had ducked under and left. The bank to the west was approximately six feet high, and a set of wooden steps led down it right at the end of our gangplank. At the top stood a neat summer cottage, now vacated, and to the south a well built wood shed with a few sticks of dry wood. But there was a prize: to the north and slightly nestled in a thick grove of quaking aspen stood a modern, state of the art, chick sales, outhouse. It had a modern chimney to the rear, all openings were screened, and there was a good quality door with locking hardware inside. There was a lift up hardwood seat with a matching cover, a fifty pound sack of hydrated lime with a scoop, and hanging on a string the inevitable Sears Roebuck Catalogue with just a few pages missing. We could use this, but we would repay the owner by watching his house.

There was an access road that ended just past this property, and looking south, we could see a house above this road and on a hill. There was smoke coming from the chimney, so we knew there would be neighbors during winter. Climbing higher, we came to the railroad with a double set of tracks, and looked for a path we could take to reach the highway and then La Crescent. This we found, and with that knowledge, returned along the railroad tracks and stumbled over a large piece of

Winter in the Shelter of the Wing Dam

coal, which we picked up and carried home. We could save that for a really cold day.

We intended to walk to La Crescent in the morning for buttermilk and knuckle bones (for the dog) so we wrote our letters, washed and dried clothes in the yet balmy breeze, scrubbed the now filthy dirty floor, aired out our blankets, and in general made our house ready for the winter to come. It was really shipshape by nightfall, and we felt content.

Morning saw us trudging to a beautiful small town set among apple groves. We were carrying our five gallon milk can between us and looking for a creamery, a general store, and the Post Office.

Well, our reputation had preceded us, and people stopped and wanted to talk. Some had even driven out the highway and watched our struggle to cross the river, swing past the wing dam, and then the miracle of swinging around below and coming to a stop. This, of course, was great food for our egos, and we basked in the momentary glory. Eventually we got our buttermilk, our bucket of bones and a bucket of fresh apples and vegetables. It was about a one mile hike to return.

That night saw a lowering of temperature, and by morning a thin sheet of ice was forming on our bay. The freeze would not be long now.

About ten o'clock the next day, I walked up the railroad to a path that led me directly to a sign, "'s Tavern", and a door which I pushed open and found a man, perhaps in his sixties, peering at me with a smile. Before I could say a word, he said, "You're one of the boys floating a house down the river. I've been watching you since you showed up across the river with your friend and your beautiful dog. But tell me, how in the world did you travel twenty-three miles through the worst and cruelest storm this part of the country has ever seen, and how did you stop when the ice was thick around you and moving fast?"

Well, we seemed to like each other immediately. He told me to call him Daley, and he was to call me Carl. He was a bachelor living alone in the back quarters of his house and was in charge of the railroad telegraph and watering station. He had opened the tavern shortly after the repeal of prohibition for something else to do and to help a certain boredom he felt. Our conversation flowed freely back and forth, and all at once he said, "You are going to have dinner with me."

Mr. Daley, owner of Daley's Tavern, stands by its front door. It is winter with snow on the ground and the Mississippi River frozen solid, as shown in the background.

Winter in the Shelter of the Wing Dam

Those days, dinner was at noon. We went to the kitchen where potatoes were already boiling on a propane table top stove, and soon he had another burner going with a large, cast iron skillet in place. Into this he put four thick, center cut pork chops from a new butcher shop-wrapped package, and when they were done, he made the best tasting dark brown gravy I have ever eaten. Needless to say, I ate like food was going out of style.

I finally got around to telling him that I played the accordion after a fashion, and if he had a good Saturday night crowd, perhaps I could bring it up and play for whatever the cup would yield. Well, he was really enthusiastic and said," You come at six o'clock and I'll have supper ready. You eat while I tend bar, then I'll eat while you tend bar." "Heck, I don't know how to tend bar or run a cash register," I said. "I'll teach you right now," he said, and he did.

On my return to the house, Clarence had various savory pots and pans going while he was studying some notes and preparing to get busy writing something again. We were settled in, and that was a really good feeling.

It was cold again that night; the ice was about an inch thick by morning. We decided to don our back packs, take our saw and ax, walk down the railroad a few blocks, then cross over a frozen back water to an island, where we could see the top of a dead oak tree from the house, our object being to find a supply of dry wood.

As we approached our tree, we heard a man already sawing wood and when he spied us, now close, he said, "Well, hello, the two boys from the river. I'm ----ski (here he pronounced a long and difficult name). Just call me Gus." A Polish immigrant, he was a U.S. soldier with one leg gone but was handling his problem very well with the aid of a strapped-on peg. He, too, had watched us through binoculars every day

Second Age

since our appearance on the opposite shore. Noting our saw and ax he said, "Boys, there's real good wood in this tree, enough for both of us for all winter. And when we have all these branches cleaned up, I'll bring my two man crosscut saw and we'll take the trunk down."

When we started to saw, he laughed, handed his saw to us, and when it cut through the wood like a hot knife through soft butter, offered to sharpen ours so it would cut like his. What a wonderful person. He had a sled with perhaps one hundred pounds of wood loaded and lashed on. We loaded our packs, and carrying our tools, helped pull his sled to and over the railroad tracks to the bottom of the hill, where we left our loads and helped him up the hill to his house with his. His wife was a buxom, vigorous, fairly heavy-boned woman with large, friendly eyes. And of course we just had to stop and have coffee and a huge piece of apple pie, and of course we just had to take home a bag of apples from barrels packed in the basement, and of course we just had to come visit soon to play cards. And, of course, we became good friends and did thoroughly enjoy many spirited card games.

Leaving our ax as well as our saw for sharpening, we retrieved our packs of wood and returned home along the railroad, where we located two more chunks of coal. We were already loaded so returned and picked them up after dumping our wood.

One time I discussed the mystery of the coal lumps along the railroad tracks with Daley. He had an astute knowledge of many things. He explained that there were many men "riding the roads", so to speak, who were unemployed, restless, looking for work, traveling from place to place more or less aimlessly. They were called different names: bums, hobos, knights of the road, etc. A hatred of the railroad and the wealth it represented was a common cause to share with each other, therefore when they rode aboard a coal car through an area populated by poor or working type people, they would become Robin Hoods and take from the rich and give to the poor. His analysis was probably not too far from the truth.

It had been dark about one and a half hours when I showed up at Daley's that Saturday night with my accordion. Already a few beer guzzlers were at the bar and animated conversation had started. Dinner was ready, and so was I. Daley stayed with me for at least a half hour, until I became more familiar with the bartending. It was so simple: lean the mug under the spigot, check for a rising bead or head, and serve with a bit of foam spilling over the side. Calculate the charge, collect, and punch into the cash register. People came here not only for beer but also for conversation, and to let their hair down and have a good time. They talked lively about mundane things, told jokes, sometimes ribald, laughed much and then turned to singing. This seemed to be the usual progression of events. The singing was my cue to go into action with the accordion, and almost at once the dancing began, and foot stomping and hooting added to the merriment.

This first night was a good one. Everyone, including me, had a good time, and my cup yielded a couple of dollars. I left my instrument there and walked home under a bright starry sky, my shoes crunching in a light snow that had come down early that afternoon. It was extremely cold and the warmth of our house from the banked fire was welcome to my tingling nose and ears.

Winter was now fully upon us, and cold prevailed night and day. The last of the ice floes had been immobilized, and they now lay snug and tight against each other, glued together by the hands of Jack Frost. Each day the ice would grow thicker and thicker as the water's heat was sucked away by the frigid air.

With the cold, our heating stove developed a ravenous appe-

Second Age

tite which lasted twenty-four hours a day. Now we made arrangements with Gus to fell our huge oak tree on the island. Carrying our lunch, a bucket of coffee, and our tools, we arrived to find him already there with a fire going a short distance away. He had brought steel wedges, a twelve pound maul (now heating by the fire, so they would not shatter in the cold) and his long crosscut two-man saw. It took up most of an hour to bring this ghastly dead skeleton down with a splintering crash. Now we fell upon the carcass with ax, saw, wedge, and maul and steadily built up a pile of stove ready wood. Using the long crosscut we began slicing neat twelve inch thick rounds from the butt end and split these with the maul. All in all, when we returned to the fire for our sandwiches and coffee, we were pleased with the wood already made up, and the huge amount yet to go.

We had brought our corrugated iron sheet, made up into a toboggan shape with pulling ropes attached, and we now loaded this with three to four hundred pounds of wood. There was about six inches of snow on the ground and only a short, downhill pull to the bay, where we could pull over the ice directly to our house. It was yet early, so we worked another couple of hours slicing off rounds and splitting them up. It was very stimulating working in close harmony together in this honest labor, in the silence of the forest where the ring of the ax or the bite of the saw was clear, distinct and clean.

Gus did not want to skid wood home that day, and we had no trouble with our load, which we stacked neatly on the porch. Our sleep was great but we awoke with sore muscles, not being accustomed to such labor.

Our days now consisted of reading, writing, and on clear days, fetching after wood. About once a week we went to La Crescent for mail, buttermilk, and large knuckle bones which we said were for the dog, but which we actually cracked for the rich marrow. I was eating more and more at Daley's on his invitation. My music continued on Saturday nights. The crowd was larger, and the cup sometimes yielded as much as five dollars. In addition there was about four hours of cleanup required on Sunday morning, so I became a Sunday morning swamper. My first morning with the first sweep up there were over five dollars laying on the floor: dimes, quarters, dollar bills dropped by the happy, careless patrons. Daley said, "That's yours." This additional income (one time it was over twenty-five dollars) swelled our nest egg and gave us a degree of independence.

Across the highway and about one hundred feet south of the tavern, was this unusual waterfall --- its movement now frozen as if it was still falling. Its summer water was sweet, cool, and delicious. With it we kept the tavern buckets full.

Second Age

Clarence had completed some poetry and needed to return to St. Paul to confer with a writers' guild he belonged to, and to make a round of his publishers to try and sell some of his work. He left the middle part of December, and it was past the middle of January when he returned. He did have some luck, though, and now had a small monthly income for the next two years.

Meanwhile, I was spending more and more time at Daley's, our home fires ran out of fuel, and the sand cooled down and was cold. The water beneath our house now froze solid around the barrels, and we were one with and in the river, a mere speck on this ice cube one mile wide and five hundred miles long, but nevertheless part of it.

Our floor consisted of two inch planking, with one layer of tar paper and then three quarter inch fir flooring. This was hardly enough to keep the icy cold out, so our feet were freezing all of the time. Our four side windows were single pane with no storm windows, so we folded the bedspreads from the upper bunks to fit the two rear ones and tucked them into a tight fit. We lost half our light by doing so. We carted home huge amounts of corrugated cardboard and placed it under our bunks and all mattresses. We also placed a few layers on the floor between our bunks, then tacked a spare Army blanket over it in place of a rug. Also, we tacked cardboard over the front and rear doors, both sides. The only place warm for our feet was the sandbox. One day we had walked to La Crosse and saw some felt boots being advertised in the J.C. Penney store window. They sure looked good, so we each purchased a pair and they turned out to be absolutely great. No more cold feet.

Now, what about Jack during this winter time? Every once in a while he would come on the house, look around and greet us profusely, then leave and vanish into the dusk. His usual time to come was just before dusk. We knew he kept close track of us because of his footsteps on the bank above us and around the cabin. On clear days one or both of us would take the twenty-two rifle and hunt either our wood island or go way across the frozen river and hunt the Wisconsin shore. His tracks would be everywhere, and we once found a bloody spot and a rabbit's ear among them.

In this manner, January and February passed, and the middle of March began with a measly hint of spring to come. Even the snow began to look warm, tired, and ready to quit its job. The river was still in a deep sleep, though a subtle change was taking place, in that the whip cracking sound of real cold ice was replaced by more of a mushy soft rumble. A few crows appeared. With the first of April a warm period arrived, and there was much speculation as to what day the ice would break up and leave. First, though, in sunny spots the snow yielded up its BTU's and became water, where crocuses suddenly appeared and blossomed. Ice along the shore began to melt, and soon we had a six inch border of water, where carp poked their heads out to look around, and we speared them at will. When carp are taken at this time from the almost-frozen water and smoked, they are excellent to eat, firm and tasty. As soon as the water warms they become inedible to most people.

Second Age

Spring Thaw

Well, the mighty Mississippi, like a bear coming out of hibernation, awoke with a start, broke its icy cover into millions of cakes, and shoved them all at one time downstream. This event then was its invitation to all the birds to return and now populate its surface, and they accepted by flying in huge noisy, busy flocks of all manner of waterfowl.

On land the meadow larks were among the first to return. Lying in our bunks at daybreak we could hear them bringing in the new day with their crystal clear, joyous song—so full of vitality, so happy. Soon robins appeared to yank wiggling angle worms, begin building nests and singing as they labored. Pheasants, crows and blackbirds were everywhere.

Our house was now floating proudly, as was its destiny, and the warm weather caused us to remove the bed spreads from the rear side windows. The room now became light and airy.

With only a few hours' warning, a heavy blizzard and snowfall came down from the north and put about eighteen inches of new snow over most of northern Minnesota. Then a day or so later, not to be outdone, a warm wind came up from the south and met monsoon winds from the northwest, and this set the skies to pouring down heavy rain for twenty-four hours or more. The result was, everything that was frozen now melted, the old ice, the new snow, the old snow, and added its water to that coming from the sky. Now ditches, pipes, waterfalls, creeks, and small rivers all dumped their load finally into the Mississippi.

Our first inkling of disaster ahead came when we found Jack asleep on our porch one morning and our gangplank too short because of rising water. We had just filled our wood box but had left a sizable amount of wood in the woodshed near the water. We decided to stay put. In an hour or so we pulled the gangplank aboard and figured we had gone up at least four feet. By three o'clock we had gone up another four feet and were now even with the bank. After supper, water was in our privy and soaking our dry wood in the woodshed. By nightfall the water had risen to the first step of the cabin and would soon enter the door. There was no turbulence where we were and all seemed quiet and peaceful. We filled our lamps and lanterns with kerosene and were happy that we now had good flashlights and extra batteries.

We decided we could nap until ten p.m. so lay down in our clothes, but it was one a.m. when we awoke and heard things swishing past the house. A beam from our flashlights showed the water now up to the top of the windows of the cabin. Debris of all kinds hurried by us in a quick rush, which told us the water was coming over the wing dam. Thank gosh our anchor cable to the tree on the top of the bank was holding stoutly, except that it now slanted downward instead of upward. Debris had collected behind our house and was putting so much pressure on the cable that it was pulling the rear of our house down into the water. Now we put our pike poles again into action, pushing the debris to the side and then preventing further accumulation. Once cleared and a lot of the pressure removed, it took only one of us to keep it so.

When good visibility returned in the morning and we had looked to the north, there was no wing dam, not even a ripple. Looking to the east, Minnesota Island was not visible. Water covered all to the

Second Age

Wisconsin bluffs. To the south, our wood island and a few tree tops were visible. The house of Gus, with smoke from the chimney, could still be seen with safety elevation to go.

To the west, the access road and railroad tracks were flooded, plus the lower parts of the highway.

And the water was still rising, but slowly now.

Standing at the back of the house and pushing off the debris was an education in itself, for we saw many things. Brush, trees, logs, boards, and plants were the main bulk. Many dead animals, hogs, chickens, cows, sheep, and even dead fish came and went. A team of two horses, still side by side, fully harnessed and with bits in their mouths slid past. A football floated on, a dead Holstein dairy cow, legs sticking out and her huge belly distended with putrefaction came up behind us, and when my pike pole came to push her aside, it penetrated her skin, and gas erupted with an evil smell. Small individual hog houses, most intact, came by as well as parts of buildings, such as a roof or a wall, still intact. What looked like a new coffin, about two hundred feet away, went south. We wondered at the time if it was occupied and if so, whether or not he could swim.

A new lock and dam at Dresback, five miles north of us, was planned for construction and toward that end there had been accumulated a huge stack of piling with which to construct a coffer dam. The high water had inundated this stack, and all at once it came tumbling down and pitched itself into the stream. Hundreds of those expensive, pressure treated black sticks now charged downstream in total disarray but were far out and were no threat to us. It was a sight, though.

The water had now reached the eaves of the cabin, yet it stood firm. Our cable was now slanting at a higher degree and was pulling the rear end of our house down a bit into the water. Our real worry though was that the cable that held us would break and leave us completely at the mercy of the river. Then when the river dropped, we might find ourselves in a farmer's cornfield two miles from the water, or on top of an island in a grove of trees, or maybe on the railroad tracks. All of these were unpleasant thoughts.

In our area the water reached its highest level at the cabin's eaves and then slowly began to recede. Less debris was coming down, but the cable was holding us directly south of the tree, and therefore we would come down on top of the embankment. We must be there to push off when the time came, and we did not know when that might be. Finally the top of the wing dam appeared, the river with its strong current was shunted aside and we were able to push off the bank and float over the approximate spot where our winter days had been spent. In time we were lowered to our original level, and our cable again slanted upward. The flood was over.

On scouting our river bank and its buildings, we discovered the cabin was completely intact, not even any windows broken. The woodshed was there, but all our wood had simply floated away. Our modern, state-of-the-art privy was gone, leaving only a water-filled hole, and with no relief in sight for us. We might just as well move on.

During the winter we had prospected and walked a waterway which would rejoin the main river just past the La Crosse bridge on Pettibone Island, where we had located a spot to tie up for the summer. We therefore unwired our hook on the cable, unloosened it, pulled it aboard, and poled toward our waterway a short distance away. We picked up a sluggish current there and waved to Gus and his wife as they stood above us and watched.

We had about four miles to reach our destination and the current was so slow we barely moved. Using our pike poles, each on a side, we placed them in the water then walked the length of the boat, pushing, then carried them forward, and walked a total of eight miles to gain four. About two feet under the water's surface, we found a rock fence or dam crossing over from side to side. Then about a mile further, there was another one, this one only about eighteen inches under. Ye Gods, the river level was falling, and we might be trapped if there were any more dams. Sure enough there was, and we barely scraped over it. The goal was barely in sight when we came to a dead stop with no clearance to pass over this final obstacle. But we jumped into the water onto the fence and rolled rocks off the top until we could make it over. Once more poling, we reached our spot and anchored, again finding a stout tree for our cable to tie up to.

This was truly a beautiful spot. The rear of our house was pulled into a growth of cattails, while the gangplank went over the side onto a grassy, gentle slope. About a block to the south the main channel flowed past, while to the east a narrow finger of heavily wooded land jutted out. We could barely hear the traffic of the bridge above and behind us, or the noise of the busy city. We were isolated and remote, yet so close to everything. It was ideal for a summer.

We cut a short winding path into heavy brush close by and there dug our hole, built our box, and nailed on our polished factory-made seat. No state-of-the-art this time, just plain utility. Later, we would build walls, roof, maybe a door, depending on what we could find for free.

Having no further need for the wood heater, we dismantled the pipe, carried the stove ashore, and removed the sandbox. After a good scrub down our house looked and felt just like it did when we first lived in it on Lake Johanna, complete with redwing blackbirds singing from the swaying cattails. A bevy of ducks was always around, and tree birds of all descriptions.

In two days we had everything shipshape and were again ready to pursue our individual lives. On counting up our pot, we were pleasantly surprised to find more than sixty dollars there. We decided to split this pot in half, then each put in two dollars every week, which would be used for food, kerosene, strictly household expenses, etc. Our personal items, shoes, socks, toothpaste, etc. we would take care of on our own. In retrospect this simple, natural act, which made sense in a subtle way, was the fork in the road where we began our adventure into our own destiny. I would never again share a money pot without reserve until I became married.

Traffic seemed to be moving over the bridge, which indicated that the roads were now open, so I hiked up through La Crescent and on to Daley's, who had noted our departure but knew where we now were. We had much to talk about. The railroad had started sending trains over its tracks that day, so he would go back on that job at four p.m. Could I take over? Yes, I could. It was Thursday; business would be slow.

The contractor on the dam had offered thirty dollars for each piling that was received from the flood and which was delivered back to them. To the river people, this was a bonanza, a ripe plum for the picking, and soon boats of all kinds were slowly churning upstream towing one, two, or whatever log pilings. This process continued for a long time, and it was said that some were towed as much as two hundred miles upstream.

Daley had a car and an old Chevrolet pickup truck. He now suggested that I use the pickup to go pick up a keg of cold beer from the Miller High Life Brewing Company in La Crosse, as needed. What a guy. I now had wheels, and he had someone readily available to fill in, hit and miss.

Second Age

Construction had now begun on the Dresbach Dam, and I had an application in there for work. A rather frail man with a crippled leg became a timekeeper there and came in after work and had a beer or two. He knew of my need and said he would look out for my interests as best he could. He was always quiet and reserved, never one to become excited. One night he had to stay overtime because of a night crew, and came in about eleven o'clock, and was sitting at the bar near the door having his usual beer. Daley had left for La Crosse to pick up another keg, for we were running low. Two men and two women had been sitting at the bar having a few beers, and they now left in their car, but in doing so, they ran into my timekeeper friend's car and dented a rear fender. While they drove off, he calmly stepped out and jotted their license number down. They apparently saw him do this because they turned around, returned, and facing him, demanded the paper back.

The two women were doing this along with much vile language, and finally one of them hauled off and slapped him hard cross the face. This set off a terrible anger in me, and I snatched a pistol from under the counter, cocked it in a thrice, and came around the bar with my finger on the trigger, and was now just a hair breadth away from committing a terrible tragedy. The two men gathered their women and left. I left by the back door and walked down the steps toward the railroad but halfway there became violently sick. It seemed that I would never stop retching, and when it was over I was shaking like a leaf and actually hating myself. Was I after all nothing but a coward, one who had to hide behind a gun?

After a time I heard Daley return and wheel a keg of beer in. Soon a car drove up, and I heard loud voices and a scuffle going on. When I weakly gained the porch and went in, there was Daley standing in the middle of the floor, one sleeve had been ripped from his shirt, and one cheek was bleeding. One of the women was laying on the floor, out cold, and the other sitting in a chair, retching and moaning while her husband was holding her head. All the fight was gone out of them, and Daley told the men to pick up their trash and get out. He then told me they had come in looking for me. One of them had slapped him, and he popped her on the chin. The other had come in like a wildcat, pulled his sleeve off, and when she scratched his face, he had kneed her in the belly. Days later, I asked how he could possibly hit a woman. He said whether it's a dog, bear, man, or woman, when they attack you, you have the right to resist.

    I, however, could not shake off the dark thoughts that were mine. The music had left my life, and the smile fled my lips. I could or I would not play for Saturday's dance, nor would I be there. In my own mind I was worthless, and this mood continued for almost two weeks. Our house in all its solitude, serenity and peacefulness did its best to heal, but the wound was deep.

    Then Daley came by and said, "Grab your hat. We're going up into Wisconsin to a Chippewa Indian pow-wow at their tribal grounds." Soon we were en route to Winona, over the bridge into Wisconsin, and north a total distance of some one hundred seventy-five miles. It had started raining lightly and was still coming down when we drove onto the grounds, where Daley's friend came out of a real bearskin wigwam and conducted us to a small cabin, where his parents lived. It was almost dark, so we moved right in and ate a light supper already prepared for us. It was now quite late, and we were tired. They indicated that we were to sleep in their bed. Daley now presented them with a very small bottle of moonshine. During the night, I woke up many times, and those two were slowly rocking back and forth before a flickering fire in an isinglass stove and crooning softly in a monotone.

    Dawn brought happy voices, and looking out the window, we

Second Age

saw about a dozen men decked out in feathers, breechcloth and moccasins, carrying quivers of arrows on their backs, knives at their belts, and carrying bows. They set themselves into a trot and soon disappeared into the trees.

A nice breakfast of corn bread, honey, wild berries, and meat we thought to be venison was brought to we four. It proved to be very tasty, and we ate it with gusto.

The village consisted of twelve one-room cabins, a fairly large meeting hall and about a dozen wigwams. The people now living in the wigwams were from all over the state. They were doctors, lawyers, clerks, laborers, etc., coming to relive, for a few days, their heritage and act out parts of it. They were good looking, tall, straight, and with strong bony head features. The women were dressed out in beaded doeskin and moccasins, while children chased each other in many kinds of clothes and feathered headbands.

They had a fire going under a huge iron pot (maybe sixty gallons). Along about noon a great cry went up, and out of the woods came the hunters with a small black bear slung on poles and carried by four braves. The women now fell upon the bear with their knives and brought pieces of meat to the pot, and tossed them in. Finally there was enough.

Daley, with his fine sensitivity to the mood of the people, now somehow sensed that these good people would be able to get into their act better if we were not there as observers. What they were doing had a certain religious meaning to them. He therefore looked up his friend and extended many thanks. Our elderly host and hostess were fast asleep on the bed, so after leaving a small gift for each, we returned home a day early. This experience broadened my knowledge of the nature of man, but on that subject there is so much to learn, and learn, and learn. It also helped me part way out of my depression.

One morning I just knew I had to walk the river bluffs above the La Crescent Valley. I therefore took our trusty single shot twenty-two rifle to Daley's, told him where I was going, then climbed from the road to above the waterfalls, where I picked up a game trail and followed it south about one hundred feet below the rim. I wasn't hunting, just enjoying the beauty of everything.

Eventually I came to a rock slide maybe two hundred feet down and about three hundred feet across. The game trail led across in a zig-zag manner, up and down over rocks, etc. I was past halfway where the morning sun now was warming the rocks, when I spied a large rattlesnake on a flat stone. He was probably still sluggish from the cold, but I didn't wait to find out. Every nerve I had was now at full power, and I moved along the trail not fast but wary, seeing a bit of movement here or hearing a slithering sound there. Believe me, I wanted more than anything else in the world to be out of that rock slide. Nearing its end, I did hear a hollow rattle behind me, but it sounded far enough away, and I emerged again into cool woodland which was too cold for my slippery friends.

The wooded area was small, and when I pushed through to the other side, there were two tall, skinny young men standing there, each holding a forked stick and a gunny sack. "Did you see any rattlesnakes coming through that rock pile?" one asked. "Yes," said I, "and you can have every single one of them." They had caught snakes before and were delivering them to a place where they milked the venom from their fangs.

Well, I kept looking at them and finally said, "Say, aren't you Beanstalk Johnson?" "Yes," he said. "Well, then, you must be Hoehandle Hogan," I said. "Then you must be Bash Franson," he said. We had been students together during our sixth grade elementary school and had given each other nicknames, theirs because they were so tall and skinny, and I because I was so bashful. Well, they were anxious to get at their rattlesnakes, and I to get as far away as possible. And so we parted, never to meet again. I took off down a farmer's wood-cutting trail, onto a country road into the city of La Crescent, and then back to Daley's. Somehow I felt better about myself.

One day a worker from the dam was at the bar and talking about some large catfish he had noticed in a cove about a mile above the dam. Next morning on leaving our house, I put our break-down fish spear in the pickup and covered it with a Bemis bag, like those used to ship one hundred pounds of seed corn. Late that afternoon, I went to this spot. Walking carefully along the shore and peering into the clear water, I thought I saw water being switched slowly around by a tail and made out the outline of a huge fish. I jammed the spear hard and the action exploded, but I had him fast and he was soon on shore, where I polished him off with a chunk of wood. We had caught many catfish on trot lines but absolutely nothing like this. When Daley checked it out, he said it was at least twice as big as anything he had ever seen come out of the Mississippi. We wrapped it in a blanket, then drove up to the waterfalls and sloshed it down real good with cold water. At four o'clock the next morning, I drove up to the back door of a butcher shop in La Crosse and he, after checking the gills, gave me eleven dollars or fourteen dollars, I don't remember which, for it. I sure wish I had a picture of that one.

Soon after, my lame timekeeper friend came in and said a job was waiting for me at the dam. Next morning at eight o'clock, I was put to work cleaning up after carpenters and taking a bucket of water around to the workers occasionally. The third day at eight o'clock, the foreman asked if I had ever fired a boiler. "Here, I'll show you what to do," he said. "Notice how much steam the pile driver is using. Watch the pressure gauge. Shovel in coal to keep the pressure up, and keep track of the water level." It wasn't hard to do, and I caught on really quickly. This boiler was on the bank, and the steam was transported to the pile driver by insulated pipes and high pressure hoses. After about ten days of this, I came to work one morning and the boiler was gone. It and the bank it was on were both in the river. They explained that in driving the piling, the river's current had been directed against the bank, and it had cut away the footing.

I was next to be a truck driver. There was cement to be poured, and a lot of it. A large cement mixer was beside the railroad track, where waiting cars loaded with gravel would be unloaded by large drag lines directly into the hopper of the mixer. Another track held cars loaded with cement, and a conveyer carried their loads to another hopper. Underneath the discharge chute, there was a set of railroad tracks, half size, which led out over the dam on a high trestle that looked mighty skimpy and in fact was a bit shaky.

The truck I was to operate was specially built. It had railroad wheels which fit on the tracks, and had only one speed forward, and the same speed reverse. It had mechanical brakes (air and hydraulic had not yet been invented), and on its back it carried a fifteen yard capacity body with a side dump gate. In operation, we would place the truck under the mixer's discharge chute and receive fifteen yards of mixed concrete, then go out on top of the trestle to a metal chute and stop at exactly the right spot. A man there would open the gate, and I would clamber up to the side of the body with a spade to push down any clinging concrete. The done and the load delivered, we would reverse to be switched to a side track while the second truck loaded and went up the trestle. Now we pulled forward off the switch track and reversed on the main line to a position under the loading chute. Round and round we went, day after day, while the dam grew. I never did feel exactly safe on this job, because I could feel the trestle trembling under its heavy load, and then the brakes were hard to apply. The brake problem I helped by slipping a pipe over the parking brake handle, which multiplied the pressure. However, I was drawing top wages and was content.

As work progressed, I developed a certain pride and satisfaction in my work, and in a sense the dam became mine. After all, it could not be built without a truck driver, or a carpenter, an engineer, a straw boss or a general manager, could it? We were all of equal value according to our abilities. Today in writing this, I wonder if we all have a need within us to become involved in some great and noble deed and be part of a group effort. It had to be some individual pride that would build the Stonehenge arches in Northern Europe, or the pyramids in Egypt, or the huge stone faces of Easter Island. I was glad that I had the opportunity to satisfy my need.

As the summer passed, I was still at Daley's maybe half the time. I still played on Saturday nights, still swamped out Sunday mornings to find more money on the floor, and tended bar a bit by filling in when needed. On Fridays after work, I usually went home. It was really very nice, sitting there in the tules, very calm, very peaceful—a time for reflection.

One Saturday, I decided to row down river about three miles to find a small inlet to a black water pond. A man had told us that we would feel like we were in Dante's hell when we got there. Well, I found the inlet and rowed into the pond. It sure enough had black water on which green and yellowish scum floated in patches. White tree skeletons stood among grayish cattails and a slight sulfur smell was in the air. Sure enough I felt a certain unease and turned the boat to row out. It was then that a large water snake came swimming toward me. I was still jumpy from my rattlesnake encounter so rested the oars, picked up the twenty-two and shot him. He was of the harmless variety but he surely was a big one. There were several more swimming around, so I rowed back to the river and home.

Jack had been with us when we tied up and then had left. There was no sign of him anywhere, and as time went on we decided he was not coming back. After all, why should he, he had waited all winter to continue his trip with us and now we were tying up for the summer. "I'll just find myself another pair of know-nothing foolish boys and take care of them," he said.

Clarence was doing well with his writing but had sacrificed a part of his hours to a part time job. He had also acquired a half blind dairy cow with a calf, and they fed on the lush meadow grass by the river. His small garden was eaten up by all manner of vermin.

We had come upon a very large snapping turtle, and when he fastened his teeth into a stick, we flipped him over on his back and skidded him home. Butchering him was an arduous task, but we gathered a large pan full of white meat which we soaked in salt water. The muscles kept twitching and making the water plink, and this kept my mother awake all night; she had come down on the bus for a two day visit.

The turtle shell and the underplate we dried and then I cleaned and cleaned and polished it. We found directions at the library how best to finish and preserve it, and now had two beautiful shells having the color and appearance of giant clam shells, but infinitely more intricate and detailed. I now set the large shell upside down on the four legs of the plate and secured it with screws, then located a filigreed gold handle from a piece of good crockery, and fitted it to the top shell with tiny screws. Sitting on our bureau, filled with fresh fruit, it was very elegant indeed. Then it was gone, stolen by somebody, and we saw it no more

Second Age

Farewell to the Floating House

The summer days sped by quickly. Moneywise I was doing really well, and saving almost everything I made. Sometimes I would even splurge by buying a haircut. I also now took my dirty clothes to a laundry: I was coming up in the world.

Daley was also doing well and was planning to expand by completing the upstairs rooms, and moving up there with the two bedrooms. An outside stairs had already been built when he changed his plans.

Autumn had now come, and we had still not decided whether to resume our trip or go back to school. Clarence had made a trip to St. Paul and when he returned, Virginia was with him, and the happy looks on their faces told me that they were now married. That pretty well settled the question of the trip.

There was another month's work on the dam before winter shut all construction down, and I dilly-dallied whether to quit then to make the first quarter or continue to work and go back to school after Christmas. I worked.

By then I had become quite a part of Daley's, and we were working more and more together. I therefore told him that I was going to leave the area when the dam closed down and would probably go back to school. He was happy because he had had a good offer by a buyer for his place and would now go ahead and sell. About two weeks

Farewell to the Floating House

later, Clarence and I got together and worked out a deal satisfactory to both, and I packed my old cardboard suitcase. It was difficult to leave our house, now theirs, but I wished the lovely Virginia and Clarence the best of the river and went to stay with Daley. We would not meet again for many years and much water had passed under the bridge.

Strangely enough, I missed most our long and sometimes heated discussions we used to have on any and all subjects. We were both reading good books and found much to talk about. I never, then or now, cared for, really liked, or understood most poetry, but prose was a different matter. We seemed to have the uncanny ability to needle each other into a fever of mental gymnastics. I think we were helping each other expand our horizons. It was great while it lasted.

Friends from up and down the river were also in my thoughts. I really liked them, they were such a colorful people, independent, resourceful, talented, and though poor moneywise, were rich in many other ways. I had learned many things from them.

Now the work of the dam shut down and Saturday came. I would play for the last dance that I was to play for in my life. Sunday morning I swamped out and hunted the floor money. I was probably the only sober saloon cleanup man who ever lived, according to western magazines, and now that job came to an end forever.

An empty bread truck from La Crosse, headed to Minneapolis for a load of fresh loaves, stopped, and I climbed on with my accordion and suitcase.

Daley had been a wonderful person to me. His sensitivity to all things around him and his uncanny ability to convert this to action continued to amaze me. Our parting was brief and warm.

It was nice to be home with the folks again. Irving was the last of ten children yet with them, and he would be leaving soon. Many of

Second Age

my former grade school fiends had married and were already into their line of life's work. I visited for hours with my mother, who took in every word, it seemed. After chores, Dad would come in and both would listen to the accordion, and they even danced a Swedish polka. It was great, but I became restless.

Second Age

Part 2

Second Age

Out to San Francisco

Two weeks or so before Christmas a letter came to the folks from my sisters, Veryne and Ollie, in San Francisco, California. It would be six weeks before the second quarter would begin at the University. "Ah ha," I said, "I'll just take a trip and visit them before school." Next day I packed the cardboard suitcase and secured it with two leather belts, not ropes—a sign of my prosperity. Once more I would walk to the Osborne Crossing and catch the Anoka Trolley to Minneapolis. I left the accordion behind. Through a cold night our bus rolled on into Ames, Iowa, where we had breakfast and transferred to one that would roll us on U.S. 40, over the prairie and mountains to the passenger ferry in Oakland, California.

Sitting beside me was a rather attractive lady, perhaps twenty-five to thirty years old. She was neatly dressed, wore a ready smile and was quite witty and knowledgeable. We stopped above Donner Lake for a stretch and a view. We also had a miniature snowball fight. Someway or somehow I asked what she did for a living. Without any embarrassment whatever she said, "I'm a hooker. I'm coming from New York and will stop here in Sacramento, then go on to Oakland." Well, it kind of shook me up for a bit, but I thought how open and above board she had to be: a wonderful quality. We then rolled into the station where we bid each other a friendly good-bye.

I was standing on the prow of the ferry bearing us from the

Oakland slip to one at the Ferry Building in San Francisco. I was wearing my new long overcoat and felt hat and was all ears and eyes in this new land. There was a sharp wind blowing in through the Golden Gate, the waters were choppy, and I thought I would freeze even in my long johns, wet cold versus dry cold.

The walk, some sixteen blocks or so, was a chance to get going again after the long ride. It was very interesting, because all was so different. My sisters lived with two older girls in a large apartment, but they had a daybed in a large closet, so I stayed there for a couple of days and got our visiting done.

About a block away, on the corner of Leavenworth and Hyde, I rented a room from a Mrs. Maier, whose husband owned a hard rock gold mine in the Sierra Mountains near Angels Camp and was gone months at a time. I think she rented because she was lonely. The room was so spacious and the furnishings so elegant, but the rent so low. I think it was my second night there. I had been walking most of the day just seeing and hearing things and the room seemed cool when I came in. I looked for the heat source. It looked like a regular steam radiator with a handle faucet at its base. I turned that faucet on, heard it hiss, then stretched out on the bed for a rest. I heard the front door open, a fast rush of someone up the steps, my door was flung open, and there was Mrs. Maier. "Get down to the fresh air quick," said she. She shut the faucet off then and we did get out. She said she smelled the escaping gas the moment the door was opened, while I smelled nothing. She had forgotten to instruct me about the heating. It was necessary to light the gas with a match at the time the valve was turned on. It could have been a tragic accident.

San Francisco was at that time a most friendly, lively, inexpensive, interesting city. I would leave my room early and walk, maybe eat fruit from a stand or breakfast at Foster's, spend most of a day in Chinatown, or on Market Street. The waterfront changed every day, and I spent most of my time there. The fishing boats, pleasure craft, passenger boats, all added to the allure of this land so different from my birth home.

And then there was the banana boat, which arrived about every two weeks fresh from the tropics with green, hard-as-rock bananas still n their stalks. I learned to get close to the sorting belt where, every once in a while, they would throw a bad stalk off and we could have it. I also learned to bring a light rope, tie it around the stalk, go to the edge of the pier and dunk it deep to dislodge any spiders from the tropics. They said they were poisonous. With this thirty to forty pound stalk on my shoulder, I walked to my room and hung it up in a dark closet. Ten days later we had yellow bananas to eat. Believe me, I was not hesitant to eat them.

Fisherman's Wharf was another spot where the odiferous crab pots were always boiling. A large crab cocktail, red sauce and all the wonderful San Francisco sour dough bread for twenty-five cents was my favorite, followed closely by their Boston clam chowder, same price.

One day, I hiked out Van Ness Avenue to the bay, past the Yacht Club, the Marina, and the Presidio, peopled by officers drilling their troops, up into the originally most exclusive area where mansions stood in grandeur among large lawns and many statues, an area now decadent and seedy, felled by the 1929 market crash. I scaled the cliffs overlooking the Golden Gate and stood beside the great guns on their massive pedestals. I walked downward now, past Sutro Baths, the skating rink, the Cliff House, and to the beach where the bathers were braving the cold waves or maybe just lying in the sand, while just across the road "Playland by the Beach" was in full swing with its merry-go-rounds, mirror house, shooting gallery, roller coaster, etc. Then I took the Geary Street

Car for five cents which returned me within a block of my room.

I had walked Golden Gate Park at least twice, but today I was visiting the still life museum where stuffed animals of all kinds were displayed in their natural environment. There were three very attractive African exhibits showing animals from there and at the bottom was a large, polished brass sign that read "Jenness Richardson, Curator".

Now for a moment I must stop and return to Minnesota. In our last year at the School of Agriculture (same as high school), Clarence had written a short children's story and named it "The Pirate Mice". To illustrate it, we caught a large rat and several mice and Jenness, being a taxidermist, mounted these all in different positions. The rat he prepared with a peg leg. We then, with the help of Clarence's sister, Nellie, made clothes for each animal. Jenness then arranged these in different formations and took pictures, as he was also a good photographer. When everything was put together, we thought we had something pretty good.

A small print shop in St. Paul agreed to print and bind three hundred books for fifty cents each. We got busy twisting our friends' arms and secured about forty orders, at two dollars each. However, only twenty were advance payments, and when we went to the printer we took the forty dollars and said we had orders for twenty more. If he would let us pick up fifty books, we would deliver the twenty already paid for, and then deliver the other twenty already sold, then pick up the rest of the books. Well, he flew into a rage and refused to deliver one single book until we brought him the full one hundred fifty dollars for three hundred books. Jenness refused to do one single thing more with that man. We could not come up with it, so returned the money advanced by our buyers and abandoned this project.

Now back to San Francisco. When I returned from the museum, I looked up his name in the phone book and called. It was him all right, living about four blocks away, and I was soon at his door. It was great meeting again. He had been sent to Africa and had captured all of the animals in the exhibit and could tell some hairy tales.

I had left my name at an employment agency. They phoned one day and asked if I could go to Monterey and wash dishes for four days. Yes, I could. I was to arrive at their office at nine a.m. the following morning, when a bus would take us to this large hotel and a convention of five thousand people, and to just take a few personal things. Working clothes, housing, and food would be provided. There were about six Gray Line large tour buses there, and as we checked in one and it was filled, it peeled out and away we went. We were all temporary help, cooks, waiters, dishwashers, wine stewards, etc.

I was one of the few who had no experience in this. We arrived at about two p.m. and were herded to our quarters, a large complex back of this huge hotel, and close to the ocean. We were each given a map and directions where to go at three p.m. to receive our orders and an outline of our work, mine at eight a.m. the following morning.

Now, have you ever stopped to think of feeding five thousand people, three times a day, and serving each dish hot and tasty? When I looked at two and one half tons of good silverware in bins on roller carts, and stacks and stacks of all kinds of crockery also on roller carts all clean and waiting in this large wash room, and learned that all would be set on tables cleaned three times that day and dirtied up, then I began to get the idea of what it was all about. I was learning many things.

Between meals we had some time off, and I walked the sand dunes and beach with my temporary acquaintances. The week passed swiftly, and we were soon on the bus headed back. Our checks (mine sixty dollars) were waiting.

On the way back, I watched out of the window where I saw the large fields and neat rows of lettuce and noted the many specially built agricultural machines at work. I vowed I would one day return to that place.

I was sitting in my room one day looking out the window and watching a truck pulling a trailer loaded with bulk oranges up Powell Street. Now Powell Street going north is a steep climb, then a cross street was level, and then another steep climb and so on until the top was reached. Close to the top he must have released the clutch too fast because the truck gave a small lurch, then the tailgate broke and the entire ten or fifteen ton load of oranges came bouncing down the street in a cascade of color. They would come bouncing down to the level cross street, almost stop and then pick up speed on the next steep decline. Then they were rolling past my window, and I was out with a sack and picking up my share. Within fifteen minutes the street was clear, and I could see people three blocks away who were picking up the last from alleys and sidewalks.

One morning I took a street car to the end of Van Ness Avenue, then a ferry across the Golden Gate to Sausalito, then a street car to Mill Valley in Marin County. Now I would climb Mt. Tamalpais, my first mountain. It was a clear, beautiful day, except for a dark cloud capping the top of the mountain, and I took a trail and started up. It was exhilarating to be back on the trail among the trees, birds, deer tracks and the prevailing quiet. Just below was a giant redwood tree (another first) and I thought how it was probably half grown when Christ was born. Up the trail some more, to stop at an open spot and look at scenery, then another huff and a puff higher to ever-widening look-sees, until almost to the cloud where I could view most of the bay, loaded with boats, then far out into the Pacific to the Farallone Islands, then up the coast, the white surf ever charging ashore and being refused entrance, retiring in

Second Age

a low ripple.

Climbing farther I was now in a cold, dense cloud and suddenly felt very alone. I did not like this feeling at all so retraced my steps to the brilliant warm sunshine, and leisurely descended my first mountain and returned via street car to Sausalito. It was early in the afternoon, so I descended to a street that was on the waterfront and ordered a hamburger, with a half loaf of sourdough French bread, a huge broiled slab of hamburger with all the trimmings—sixty-five cents.

Across the street there were three floating piers held in place by piling in neatly driven rows and projecting out into a smaller bay protected by a finger of land.

To these floating docks, perhaps forty or more houseboats were tied up and together they would rise and fall with the tide. All the houses were built on flat bottom scows, and some were very old and some quite new.

The people, I was told, were of the arty world and were somewhat different. They were independent and free minded, doing their own thing as they saw fit.

In two days there would be an art show up and down the street and these people were out on their decks getting ready for their parts. Painters were dabbling on their canvas, a music group was tooting their horns. A wood carver sat among his shavings and whittled some more. A glass blower had his flame going. But toward the outer end of the middle dock a tall, good looking muscular man with red hair was practicing reciting a poem for the art show. I moved closer and all at once recognized the poem he was reciting. It was one written by John Masefield, poet laureate of England. It was one I had liked and memorized while in school.

I must go down to the sea again,
To the restless sea and the sky,
And all I ask is a tall ship,
And a star to steer her by,
And the wind's song, and the wheel's whip,
And the white sails aflying,
And a grim smile on the sea's face,
And a grey dawn abreaking.

He would recite this and then clap his hands, which caused the sea gulls to lift into the air from their perch on the piling, with a raucous cry. They were his only audience until I arrived. Then he would repeat the verse when the gulls had landed again.

Crossing back over the bay, I arrived home completely filled with the events of the day. It was sure great to be alive and to be young, well, that was heaven.

Second Age

The President Coolidge

It had become somewhat of a ritual at the rooming house to sit at the kitchen table and visit with Mrs. Maier over a cup of coffee or tea. She and her husband had followed gold mining together all over the west, including Canada and Alaska, and she had a knack of telling each experience with a mixture of humor and homey expression. For instance, her husband had smelly feet; no, they weren't smelly, they stunk, and she suggested he bury them. When going to bed he would take off his shirt, lower his pants, sit on the bed, take off his shoes, slip off his pants, then take off his socks and quickly slip his feet under the covers. An Indian in Yellowstone Park suggested that he soak his feet in the black mud of a sulfur pool. This he did and was cured. He didn't have to bury them after all.

We were visiting thus one day when I said I was not going back to school, but that I would sure like to get a job on a ship and see some foreign places.

"Why," she said, "my nephew is a purser on the President Coolidge and the ship is due in tomorrow. He comes to see me every trip, but I'll leave word for him to call or come as soon as he gets here." Well, he called, and when he came he brought word that I was to report to the head steward on the morrow and that the ship would leave that evening for Los Angeles with me aboard. I could hardly believe my good

The President Coolidge

luck but the boarding pass in my hand was convincing.

Mrs. Maier was quite familiar with what I would need in the way of clothes, which was not much, because they furnished all the ones we worked in. She also insisted on my leaving all my things just as they were, including my old cardboard suitcase, substituting instead a small handbag. I must see her in two months, she said.

I wrote and mailed a quick letter to my folks telling them of what had transpired. I called my sisters and was at the dock, passed into the ship and at the steward's desk at nine a.m. First I must join the union. (He was waiting. He came aboard every trip to collect from old members and sign-on new members if there were any.) I now signed the ship's log (known commonly as signing on) and was then shown to my quarters and assigned a bunk.

I had signed on with the Dollar Steamship Lines. They were owned by the Stanley Dollar family, and they had many ships traveling around or to and from many of the world's ports. It was also known as the President Lines because every ship carried the name of an American president.

I was on the President Coolidge and her sister ship was the President Hoover. Both would travel to Hawaii, Japan, China, and the Philippines, to turn around at Manila and return, same ports of call. These two ships were the newest, the largest, and the most luxurious of the fleet and were known as the twin jewels of the Pacific. Each would carry first and second class plus steerage passengers. Huge stacks of mail, cotton, tightly baled hay for Japan, merchandise of all kinds would fill its holds, and crude oil loaded at Wilmington, California, just out of Los Angeles, would fill its tanks or bilges.

My work was to keep the brass polished—door knobs, railings, hand rails, etc., squeeze fresh orange juice, and set up deck chairs on nice days. In the stewards' department it was considered the lowest of the low jobs, but the excitement and fascination of this entirely new life kept me at it with enthusiasm.

Now at three in the afternoon, two tiny (in comparison to us) tugboats arrived, sailors cast loose the mooring lines and very slowly and gently we were nudged away from the pilings by these tiny tugs and pushed into the bay with our prow pointed to the sea. A pilot, who had just come aboard, now took over to guide us safely to the open water. A quiver ran through the ship as the thirty ton, three blade propeller, sunk in thirty feet of water, began to turn and we began to move. Somewhere ten knots south off the Farallone Islands a boat picked up the pilot and our captain now took over full command. The Continental shelf lay five, up to ten knots from shore and this caused waves of various sizes to erupt from the deeper waters, and in turn caused a very slight roll of the ship. This was a good time to acquire sea legs.

Before leaving San Francisco, quite a party of movie people had boarded and were in first class quarters. The bar had opened as soon as we were three miles out (no tax on liquor served on the open sea) and cigarettes were now fifty cents a carton (no tax). From reports I heard I guess they had quite a party.

I spent most of that evening getting acquainted with other members of the stewards' group in our quarters, which were located forward on the port side and close to the water line. Steel pipes ran from floor to ceiling, then lengthwise to form a parallelogram, which spring-loaded steel bands spanned, on which a two and one half inch pad or mattress was placed, and this was our bunks, two per space, top and bottom. At the bottom of each bunk were two steel bins with locks named foot lockers, and this is where we kept our personal things. My bunk was a bottom one and right next to the ship's skin, sheets of two inch thick

The President Coolidge

high-tensile steel butt-welded to each other and riveted to huge steel beams. About sixty men were thus housed in a relatively small space. There was a constant hiss of fresh air, either hot or cold as needed, and this, plus the muted ship's noise, and the friction of water past the ship's skin, actually lent a comfortable touch to the atmosphere. Now berthed at the Wilmington, California, docks and hooked up to fuel oil lines, we had the day off while the bilges were pumped out of sea water (used for ballast) and refilled with crude oil.

Three of us took a street car to Long Beach and strolled around a park. We walked up to a fence around a large swimming pool. A lot of kids were looking through the fence. A man yelled from the pool, "Any of you kids want to come in swimming, come around to the front." A man came out of the pool to pay their way in, not twenty feet from me. The man was Jack Dempsey, retired Heavyweight Boxing Champion of the World. A thrill it was.

I went back to San Francisco that night. The next morning found the warehouse on the dock stacked with goods of every description. The hatches were removed and set aside, the derrick arms freed from their locks, hooks with dangling nets lowered over the side, and the work of filling the belly of this monstrous ship began, amidst much signaling and shouting of the longshoremen. They would continue all that day, all that night, and until noon the next day, when the hatches would again be battened down, the derrick arms folded and locked into place, and the ship made ready to challenge the sea.

At one p.m. passengers started to arrive in droves and with loads and loads of baggage, and there were going away parties in practically every cabin. Flowers, gifts, and champagne ruled the afternoon. At three forty-five p.m., the bellboys and I were given chimes, and our job was to be sure all visitors left. We therefore paraded every hallway, striking our chimes and announcing, "All visitors ashore." At some noisy cabins, we knocked on their doors to be sure they got the message.

Soon our two busy little tugs appeared, the gangplank was pulled in, the side door pulled shut and bolted snugly into place with long wrenches. The sailors cast off and again we were gently nudged out into the bay. A crowd was on the deck yelling and waving, while streamers of confetti draped down from every deck, and kisses were thrown with abandon. Good-bye. Good-bye.

The tugs soon had us positioned prow forward, the pilot was again aboard, the mighty propeller began its revolution, and we were off to lands completely foreign.

We were out just past the Farallone Islands when the sun shot its last rays into San Francisco. It seemed that every window there reflected each ray and became a giant blaze of white color. They said this happened very seldom, and we had just received its best.

When I went upstairs to work the following morning, there was not a speck of land in sight, and the ship was nicely slicing through fifteen foot swells with just a barely perceptible roll. However it was enough, and I barely made it back to my quarters before the heaving started, and I was seasick. Being so is a terribly bad feeling, and at times I really didn't care if I lived or died. This continued that day, all night, and until the middle of the next afternoon. Two days were gone, but the next day I went at my brass polishing with a will.

On the morning of the fifth day, the get up lights came on at four a.m. instead of the usual five a.m. We were coming into Honolulu and would come into the breakwater at precisely the moment the rays of the rising sun would appear. The Royal Hawaiian Band of sixty pieces would be on the roof of the Hawaiian Sugar Company's warehouse roof, and a native Hawaiian lady, who had greeted every arriving ship from the east for twenty years, lifted her beautiful clear, birdlike voice to sing "Aloha" (Welcome to the Islands).

I had been serving coffee and breakfast rolls to the early risers, but when the first strains of music came floating across the water I lost all my customers, so went to the rail with them. Sharks were swimming just outside the breakwater and snapping up anything thrown to them. As we edged into the bay, Hawaiian swimmers came out and climbed up the ropes thrown to them, from the very top deck. Passengers would show them a silver dollar and throw it into the bay, whereupon they would dive about ninety-five feet down and usually reappear with the dollar in their teeth.

But the moist, not too warm gentle air, the grass skirt music, and the lady with her song were so incredibly beautiful that I just stood there covered with goose bumps and deeply moved.

We now anchored at a cement wall, our gangplank went out onto a lawn, and passengers walked onto green grass, there to be greeted by a small ukelele band singing island songs, and many grass skirt clad girls bearing newly made flower leis which were placed upon passengers' necks, along with a hug and a squeeze. These girls were so childlike and seemed so sincere that I envied our passengers. But then our tasks were done, and we were free to walk down the gangplank, and there were these beautiful people, and their leis, and their music. They treated us as equal with our passengers, and we spent the next three hours with them, bedecked with leis, our shoes off and weaving around with great merriment on the grass and the shore sand.

We would leave the first thing in the morning, but many went uptown in this lovely land, and dinner was light. The head steward hunted me up and said the man I had replaced did not like his bellboy job and wondered if I would switch with him. I sure would like that, so I

Second Age

signed new ship sign-on papers and was now a registered bellboy, with no experience at all. I would now gain access to any point on the ship and had a chance to earn tips. This might double my income to sixty dollars per month and also open up many opportunities for adventure. Considering my two days off with seasickness, I had polished brass for two shifts only.

Our bellboy station was between the kitchen and the dining rooms, where a large electric board with a light was displayed for each cabin. When a passenger needed something, they would press a button and on would go the light. A bellboy would see this, reach over and switch it off, then go to answer the call. We reached each deck by means of a stairwell, seven steps up, a platform, turn forty-five degrees, seven steps, and you were up one deck. When I first began and had a call from, say, five decks up, I would arrive at a cabin completely out of breath, but after a few days I could go up two steps at a time at full speed and hardly notice a fast breath.

Soon I became buddies with the other bellboys. Tom Doyle, for instance, was much like myself, always interested in something new. His brother was a boxing promoter in Los Angeles, and Tom did not like that type of thing. Andy Gump was the son of the "Gump's" store owner in San Francisco; he was wealthy, but he was seeking something more, and he would find it, I was sure. Red Mason was a union labor enthusiast of the first order but unwilling to serve on a goon squad, and there was a dark, bearded, heavy set, rather slouchy Hiram Epstein, with a sharp mind but poor personality traits. There were others, but these four were my closest associates.

From Honolulu we sailed for eight days to Yokohama, Japan, my first experience with a land completely foreign. There was no English spoken here, and everything was different: architecture, transportation, clothing, people and streets.

Here, medical doctors examined all passengers and crew who went ashore. We stewards were lined up on the promenade deck, and a Japanese doctor and his assistant started at the end of the line. We dropped our pants to our shoes and our shorts to our knees. He selected a wooden tongue depressor and checked our throat, then used the saliva laden stick to poke our privates about, then discarded it in a bag carried by his assistant. This was known as the short arm inspection.

There were about ten of these doctors who came aboard for this work, and they began to drift into the dining room around eleven thirty a.m., but now they brought their entire families, kids, grandmas, and pas, and, I think, maybe uncles and aunts. Special menus in Japanese were provided, and I can tell you, they ordered and received the best we had, compliments of the ship. We had been instructed to give them what they wanted in a courteous manner, even though, as one of the waiters said, we had been "peter whipped and splashed with our own saliva".

Our stay was short in Yokohama so we sailed on to Kobe. Here we unloaded our crude oil from California and refilled the tanks with sea water for ballast. Tom, Red, and I wandered uptown window shopping and marveling at all and everything so different. Eventually we came upon a tea shop and entered. A carefully dressed waitress brought us out dainty tea cups on dainty saucers, and we sat there enjoying really good tea. There was a picture of a banjo over a door, and I was told that would be the toilet. I entered and found the urinals stuck out from the walls as do many of ours in public places. I was standing over one doing what I came for when our waitress came in, walked to one beside me, pulled up her skirts and stood over hers. I told you things were different here.

Many American Indian tribes had sweat houses for cleaning

themselves. Northern Europeans had their Finnish baths, the French their spas and the Dead Sea the noted hot mineral baths. In Japan they seemed to have public bath houses everywhere and these were a revered part of their culture.

Tom, Andy and I decided to go to one of these and experience what nude public bathing really was. When we arrived, my bashfulness had just defeated my resolve. They went in, but I, very unhappy with myself, sat down outside and watched the people passing to and fro. Many of the streets and narrow alleys were paved with cobblestones and these energetic peoples were forever washing and rinsing them. To keep their feet dry, many of the ladies wore wooden shoes having inch-high cleats, under the sole and under the heel, and as they walked with short steps there was a steady click-clack on the cobbles.

Here, children are playing outside their school.

Any person on their first visit to a foreign land should be in awe of the people and their culture. Here, ladies are walking along the street wearing their wooden, cleated shoes and kimono dresses.

This is a picture of a typical Japanese child.

Most of the ladies wore colorful kimonos with their hair carefully piled high on their head. Children were well groomed and dressed and played quietly up and down the alley. Men wore rather drab cotton shirts and pants with sun hats made out of reeds for it was summer and warm.

Upon my friends' return, they reported their experience as follows: The bathing pool or tub was round, twenty-five to thirty feet in diameter and filled with hot water. There were fifteen to twenty people, all nude, sitting around this pool or lying in the water. They seemed to be families who knew each other. They all seemed happy---children being loved and kissed.

After soaking for a short time, Tom and Andy sat on the pool's edge and an attendant knelt down beside each and scrubbed them from head to toe with a small brush and soap. Then they rinsed them off with a wooden bucket of hot water. Lying on their bellies, the attendants toweled them down with hot, wet toweling. After kneading their back and neck muscles, the bathing was completed.

I was surely sorry to have missed this wonderful opportunity to better know this age-old culture and vowed I would not miss the next time, but the next time never came.

This is a finely crafted zig-zag bridge, which spans a canal and leads into a temple. (You shake off the devil on the way in.)

Yokohama had many canals and this necessitated many foot bridges as well as others for bicycles and wagons. Also, many canals were gracefully curved through small, open areas or parks with a certain shy loveliness of character. Instinctively, one knew that these people honored and respected their land.

Second Age

Through the Inland Sea

Now we sailed down the inland sea, between Japan and China. There were literally hundreds of square-rigged, one-sail boats crossing over or up and down both shore lines. These vessels were called "junks", some thirty to forty feet long and steered from the rear by one single curved oar. When there was no wind, they could wiggle this oar like a fish's tail and move forward slowly. Whole families would live an entire life aboard, buying, selling or transporting merchandise.

Leaving the island of Japan, we moved south within sight of the Chinese shore until a large body of yellow water came in sight. This was the Yangzte or the Yellow River, emptying its load of silt taken from the belly of this great nation. This yellow stain on the ocean's surface reached out fifty miles from the nearest land, and it became more yellow as we pushed toward the river's mouth and up it to the city of Shanghai, where we anchored at a huge floating dock in the middle of the river. Lighters would ferry us every fifteen minutes to the city. American gun boats had escorted us in, mainly to clear the way, but also to patrol a fifty mile stretch of the river.

There was a terrible hunger upon this land from poor crop yields. We had barely tied up when they had catch nets over our sewer discharge outlets and were scavenging every bit of food they could find. We bellboys from our porthole would toss a hard biscuit out, and it was painful to see them scramble for it.

One boy in particular had grabbed a bun and had it in his mouth when a man hit him hard on the back, and when the bun popped loose he snatched it and swallowed it without chewing.

No person will ever fully know how truly terrible famine is until close to it, to hear, see, smell, and feel it.

It was ten p.m. when three of us were free of the ship, ferried ashore and went to see the sights. Directly up from the ferry slip was a paved street, and in its center a raised platform with a solid wall around it, and on which there were three Sikh guards, each armed with rifle and pistol. Standing on the street were two more with heavy clubs and pistols. These Sikh guards were big, almost black, heavily bearded and with turbans carefully wrapped around their heads. Directly across this street or plaza stood the world famous Cathay Hotel, and lined up along both sides of the street were rickshaws and their tough Chinese pullers. They were the taxi cabs of Shanghai and would take you anywhere in this gigantic city at a jogging pace. Someone said they could pull fifteen miles on a quarter cup of rice versus one and one half gallons of gasoline for our cabs.

Three blocks up the street was a huge neon lighted building (neon tubes outlined the windows, doors, corners, and a high tower on top). It was very impressive. It was known as the amusement building, and for one fee of thirty-seven cents, we were admitted. Each floor was divided into four theaters, and there was something different going on in each one: a play here, Japanese Sumo wrestling there, boxing, music, swimming, group bathing sans clothing, exercise classes. We watched a small part of each performance as we worked our way upward. Five floors up, and at the last, a wide stairway led to the roof and of all things, "The Market for Wives". Here under the stars we were seated at ceramic tables on ceramic benches. In fact, all the vases, floor tiling, and flower pots were all ceramic done beautifully in intricate designs.

A pot of hot tea laced with oily coconut butter was brought, along with dainty cups and saucers. There were quite a number of other people there, mostly men and mostly non-Chinese.

Now the child bride would appear dressed in beautiful rich silks, a face white with rice powder, and hair done up in a high pug to display the loveliness of her neck. They all seemed so fragile and child-like. Directly behind her came her mother, dressed in the filthiest of rags, usually thin and haggard looking. They would walk once around on a plush red rug and stop. A man then came out and tried one language after another, each time holding up a hand asking if there was anyone interested. If anyone was interested, he would go there immediately and start the inevitable haggling. If an agreement was reached he would signal the mother, and on her consent, would collect full payment then and there, take his percentage and hand her the balance. The child bride would return to the preparation room, return all the rented silks, don her rags, and when the buyer came by would follow meekly in his footsteps. The mother would return with some cash and one less mouth to feed. I had read somewhere that "the more people there are the cheaper life becomes". Even today it would be well to ponder this thought.

It must have been one o'clock in the morning when we emerged to a relatively quiet street. A honey wagon was slowly passing, moved by a dozen or so men pulling, and six or seven pushing.

An oriental honey wagon was simply a thousand gallon wooden tank covered, but with a dump in gate on the top and a dump out valve on the bottom. It was slung between two large steel rimmed wheels, and two stout shafts extended to the front and were held in place by crossbars. The pullers pushed against these crossbars while others used a chest harness tied to the shafts. They would park this contraption, then each would grab a honey bucket, go to the night soil and slop jars, fill their buckets, return and dump into the top gate. In this manner dozens of them would haul out to collecting points everything that we would send in our sewers. Boy, oh boy, did it smell.

Late in the afternoon a dark person in a turban was standing on the dock and was trying to sell some opals, which he displayed in his hand on a dirty handkerchief. One opal was coal black, at least three quarters of an inch long in its oval shape, and red fire was running through it everywhere. He asked thirty five dollars for it but would take thirty two dollars if I would hurry up. I had twenty five dollars, and Tommy had five dollars. I rushed back, but he would not accept the thirty dollars. He had no more time and disappeared. I sure did want that stone.

We now returned downriver through the yellowish water, escorted again by gun boats. Far from land we turned south and soon returned to green sea water. It was then that the ship pumped out one tank and several Chinese climbed through a service door on the top. They had been hired in Shanghai for temporary work; their job: clean, scrub and remove every speck of crude oil, so that these tanks could be filled with coconut oil from the Philippines and hauled to San Francisco. Air, steam, and electricity was piped to them. Detergents, brooms, or whatever was needed was furnished. They worked, absolutely naked, for two hours, then came out completely covered with oil, leaned against the companion way rail and went to sleep standing up. It took ten to twelve hours to clean each tank, and before they entered the last shift, they had soaped and showered and were clean. The last tank was clean by the time we reached Manila.

Steaming ever southward, we came to the estuary of the Wang Po River and ran up it a short distance, to tie up at Kowloon, directly

Second Age

Transportation of goods and people was mostly walking, bicycling, pulling or pushing high-wheeled carts by manpower, or carrying two baskets balanced on a springy bamboo pole. By a large margin, however, travel and transportation was by waterway. Even the small ditches and creeks had boats in them, constructed to fit the job. These pictures, taken from the foredeck, illustrate the countless thousands of those plying their trade.

Through the Inland Sea

Here is a laden barge making its way upstream. Four men are operating a long sweep or oar that moves in the water like a fish's tail. I took this picture at about 3 p.m. one day and the next day at three, the barge had not moved over an eighth of a mile. This despite the men on board who worked hard and constantly.

In the rivers, bays, backwaters, or any place where they would not interfere with thru-traffic, we found these clusters of water craft. They were tied to each other and extended far out from shore. People were born on these boats and lived their lives on them. Manny of them were craftsman, somewhat like Gypsies, and peddled their wares wherever the water would take them.

Second Age

The rules and regulations by which they governed themselves in this teeming mobile population must have been different than those on land and would be interesting to study.

across the bay from Hong Kong. Here our stack of cotton was unloaded by hand, and I was to see strong, burly Chinese longshoremen bend under a six hundred and fifty pound bale of cotton placed on their backs, begin a sing-song and carry this bale up two decks on sloping ramps, and take it to a pile on the covered dock, then return for another.

The streets of Kowloon were packed with small manufacturing shops of all kinds: pottery, dishes, statues, and one shop was carving teakwood chests, lined with camphor wood. Two boys, who looked like they were twelve to fifteen, sat teeter-totter on a wide teak wood board placed on a saw horse. The master carver drew a straight line in front of each boy across the board and told them what he wanted carved. And without any design whatsoever each would begin on his side and meet in the middle with a carved figure in perfect harmony. They did this with crude tools made mostly out of worn out wheel rims. Other workers fitted the pieces together, installed the lining, and applied the finish. Then when the hinges were screwed on and a brass harp lock installed, it became a very beautiful piece of furniture.

I measured the space under my bunk and ordered two as a gift to Veryne and Ollie, who had done so much for me, ten dollars each one, to be picked up on the return trip. On my second trip I would order two more and ship these to Minneapolis for Amelia and Wallace. Irving and Ben were not yet married, nor was I, so we three missed out.

One day we walked upriver on the Kowloon side, past pretty little bamboo houses, neat little rice patches, tiny plots of vegetables, and cucumber vines falling from flower boxes in the windows. People were utilizing every square inch of soil and every sunbeam. Maybe three miles up on this worn path we came to a bay just off the river and noticed many boats with the owners in the water. They would dive down for something, come up, throw it into the boat, then dive again. Those near shore would take their find to shore and place it in baskets. We learned that we were in the "Land of the Lotus Eaters", and they were harvesting roots that looked similar to ginger roots. All up and down this river they would now be harvesting, so our information sheet read.

Second Age

Our ship's photographer had a never-ending appetite to snap pictures of interesting people. On several occasions I walked the streets and alley ways with him in search of food for his camera. These portraits and the one on the previous page were all taken one day in Kowloon, China.

Under the Southern Cross

Leaving Kowloon we moved deeper into the tropics. Nights, now traveling under the Southern Cross, were so beautiful. Andy and I carried our pillows to the forward deck and finding a place, we laid down next to the neatly coiled hawser ropes and deck machinery. Many Chinese workers had the same idea, and their sing-song chatter went on forever. It was all so utterly pleasant just lying there, feeling the pulse of the ship, the gentle air, the sing-song talk, the smell of rope, and scrubbed oak planking.

One night the lonely ocean was absolutely smooth. No wind stirred up even a tiny wavelet. The music and dancing was over and at about eleven p.m. most passengers and crew were abed. Tommy and I were almost asleep on our blankets and pillows on the fore deck, bathed in moist, friendly and caressing air. The night was dark.

And then it happened. Three short, strident whistle blasts cut the still night air. In a flash, the entire crew was up and racing to their assigned posts and duties dressed in whatever clothes they woke up in. I arrived quickly at my post---the starboard side of the ballroom. My duty was to cover the port holes with heavy cast iron covers. My partner was one of the cooks and we had practiced the routine together. Each cover weighed about one hundred twenty-five pounds and had two slotted bars. We lifted these covers into place, then pulled two large eyebolts

Second Age

from the wall and swung these into the slots of the cover, then spun the wing nuts tight. The ship was still steady at this point but as we were rechecking the wing nuts for snugness, we felt the ship rise, then fall rapidly and tilt starboard perhaps ten to fifteen degrees. Then a loud noise crashed as the second wave took a mighty slap at the starboard side of the tilted ship. Meanwhile, the helmsman had spun his wheel hard to starboard, the propeller and rudder had done their job and by the time the third wave came in, we were cutting directly into it and were again masters of our ship.

All of this came rushing out of the black darkness and it was only the instinctual and gut-quick decision and action by the captain and his crew that held damage to a minimum. It was theorized that a gigantic underwater explosion was the cause.

In about thirty minutes the ocean was again calm, our course was returned to its original route and we plowed onward into the yet black night.

When Tommy and I returned to the foredeck we discovered that it had been savaged by the second wave. Everything was dripping wet and our pillows and blankets were gone---donated to Davy Jones' locker.

A lady and her daughter quartering on the last deck up on the ship had unknowingly left a porthole half open. That big wave we felt had reached into this hole, shattered the thick glass and drenched the room with salt water---sixty-five feet above the water line.

We stayed most of a week in Manila, where the last of our passengers disgorged. There were ships from many nations also tied up, and one day a steward from a German ship invited us aboard and showed us their complete brewery, and served us a glass of warm beer.

The weather was nice and the ships' crews went on the dock

and visited one another if language permitted. Our stewards somehow would acquire pounds of dairy butter to trade with the Russian sailors for vodka. I saw these Russian sailors sit on a box and with a pocket knife slice off and consume a whole pound of butter at one sitting.

We had visited with a rather slim and likeable bellboy from an English ship. One day Tommy and I asked him to go into Manila with us and get a milkshake. The milk added to the ice cream was from a water buffalo (they told us proudly) and was extremely rich. We were within two blocks of the ship, walking along a path above the breakwater, when it hit us, the sharp cramps in our stomachs. Tommy and I took off for the ship as fast as we could to try to avoid the impending disaster, and we almost made it, but not quite. We were, however, close to clean clothes. When we asked him the next day how he made out, he said in his English idiom, "Well, I ran for a while, and then I saw I was not going to make it, so jumped in the rocks, poked my bloody arse into a fifty mile gale and came away without a speck." Well said, I thought.

Our head chef had his desk in a corner of the kitchen just behind our bellboy chairs. He was taking a stroll on the dock in the shade of the ship, so I fell in step and we visited. He was from Minneapolis, born there, went through high school, then two years at Dunwoody Institute, a trade school where he learned to be a chef, then up through jobs until becoming a hotel chef in New York City, then losing a loved wife, then coming to San Francisco and signing on the Dollar Lines two years ago. Minnesota was a common bond for us, and he said I must eat at his desk once in a while. Now he loved to get into the pots and pans and would prepare the most fantastic meals one ever heard of: tender aged fillets, prime rib, pheasant under glass, goose liver pate, suckling pig, Turkish hazelnut pie with amaranth, most with French names. He served the soups, salads, appetizers, gravies, vegetables, and desserts at his desk on a clean, white tablecloth. This would continue for the next five months, approximately once a week. After one such feast I was laying on my bunk, hands behind my back, and looking at the sagging springs above me. Less that a year ago I was sitting down at a table with Clarence and eating buttermilk soup with rice and raisins, or maybe baked beans with cornbread. With our robust health and sharp taste buds then, I believed that plain food tasted equally as good and was consumed with much more gusto.

It was the day before we were to begin our return journey, and one of the young waiters asked if we would like to go with him to a dime—dance hall on the other side of Manila. Four of us left the ship around nine p.m. to get a taxi for the trip, but on the way a neon sign read "Poodle Dog Bar". Someone suggested that a little oil to limber our sea legs and make our feet nimble would be in order, so in we trooped.

The owner came over and suggested his special, which was prepared as follows: he would mix small portions of light and dark rum, some already fermented coconut oil, a dash of gin, rice wine, and then secret herbs and spices, and mix all this with crushed guava, wild finger-sized bananas, and papaya fruits. This mixture he would pour into a fifteen gallon staved wooden barrel and pound the bung in tightly. Then, by means of a rope, they would elevate this concoction to the top of a palm tree and lash it in place for six months.

The gentle movement of the palm trees and even temperature would cause the ingredients to fight each other and get rid of their meanness and then would come to love each other and to blend together with common purpose. When he lowered this cask to the ground and removed the bung, he would find the liquid in perfect harmony. All these things he told us. He would now frost the glasses, add ice and rum, then add a dollop of the above elixir. If we would drink three he would present us with a certificate that we were members of the "Poodle Dog Connoisseur's Club" and had passed all the entrance requirements. Little did we know what a delayed wallop this mild, pleasant liquid would hand us.

My certificate is inserted here as evidence of my stupidity.

> **Certificate of Membership**
> IN THE
> **POODLE DOG CONNOISSEURS CLUB** *Manila, P. I.*
> WALTER B. OAKES, EXALTED MASTER.
>
> Know All Men:
> That, on the 13th day of April 1935 Carl A. Tronson of Fred. Coolidge, did consume, drink, absorb and retain the total of (13) Super-Mixed Singapore Gin Slings; And, That he is therefore a life member of the Poodle Dog Connoisseurs Club, and, is entitled to all rights, privileges and courtesies due members of the Club
> Sig. Walter B. Oakes
> WALTER B. OAKES, EXALTED MASTER

Our spirits were high as we left the taxi, entered the hall, bought a dollar's worth of tickets, picked out a girl and whirled away. Did I say picked out a girl? Each girl was attended by her mother who was richly attired in white, starched mantilla lace worn over silk or satin gowns. It was to her you presented your ticket and when she had taken your cap and maybe straightened your tie, then you could dance with her daughter. It was strictly first class. It must have been the sixth dance when I left this conscious world and entered one for many hours of which there is no memory or recall. I had four dance tickets left, I later discovered.

I awoke to the sound of a pig grunting and some hens clucking, and found myself on a reed mat placed over a bamboo floor. Near the door a young girl sat cross legged on a small mat, and when I sat up, she pushed a grass door aside and left. In spite of a terrible headache, I checked my belongings. I was completely dressed and my shoes were on. My billfold was intact, and my captain' cap was beside me (my cap was just like the captain's, but no braid or stars), and my watch said twelve thirty. I was in a single room framed out with bamboo and roofed with reeds. The floor was raised four or five feet above the ground, and here was where the pigs were rooting, and I could smell them through the cracks in the bamboo floor, which was very slippery and hard to walk on in my dancing shoes.

Now pushing the grass mat aside I saw twenty or twenty-five people standing in an opening among eight or ten houses similar to mine, and they were all looking at me. Surrounding us all was a dense jungle, and I had no idea where I was or how or when I got there. The ship was to leave at four p.m. Now it was after twelve. Going down the ladder, I approached them and said, "English, English." No response. I took off my cap and pointed to it and then at my watch. Nothing. Now I knew what it was like to be a monkey in a zoo, looked at but not spoken to.

They understood quite well, however, and soon a person standing apart from the rest motioned to me to come with him, and soon an old pickup approached on a rutty road and stopped. A pair of chickens were hanging live upside down from the arm of the mirror, and a crated pig rode in back with several shy children sitting on the floor. I sat on the tailgate. We came to a better road and soon were driving past the now quiet dance hall and thus into the heart of Manila, where I disembarked and made my way to my quarters just in time to don my bellboy outfit and carry the chimes for "all visitors ashore". Now all four had returned.

My two buddies became too drunk to dance so forgot all about me and taxied back to the ship. The waiter stayed to the end, and thinking I had gone back also, had returned by himself. My hangover lasted for two days, and it would be many a moon before I touched one single drop, and many, many years before I slipped out of the conscious world for a time.

We left the Philippines with a full compliment of first class passengers, many of whom would disembark at Hong King or Shanghai, but we would pick up others. After all, we were the jewel of the Pacific, and everybody wanted to sail with us.

One such man was Frank Buck, whose book portrayed him as the great white hunter, tamer of the jungle, a man who could catch and pen the wild creatures single-handed, a man who could meet a zoo's every order. He must have had forty or fifty small animals in cages on the very top of the ship. The cover sheet of his book showed him in jungle boots, knee length tan cotton pants, a matching tan jacket with six pockets, and a pith helmet. This outfit he wore day after day, indoors and out, and was strutting and parading whenever he thought people might be looking. We people in the stewards' department did not like him one bit because of his disdain toward those who served. He treated his caged animals worse yet, and even though he had a helper to care for them, they often went without water and were not covered when the storms came or when we left the tropics for the cold winds of Japan. But he was famous, we were not, so who would best judge.

I have been so busy telling about myself that I should now say something more about the ship. I spoke about the role of the tug boats and the local pilots on entering or leaving port. This process was repeated every port we visited.

The large First Class dining room was also used as a dance hall, and we had a good five piece orchestra who played background music at dinner. Sometimes there was a special afternoon matinee, and then twice each week was party time and a dance. The piano player also played accordion in the bar late afternoons. All of the rooms were taken care of by Chinese housekeepers who were hardly noticeable as they flitted along the hallways in flowing while silk shirts, black silk billowing pants gathered at the ankle, and soft cloth shoes. They all lived together in the bow of the ship and cooked and ate their own food there. There was a fully equipped laundry manned by Chinese, and from it we drew a freshly laundered, starched and pressed, white uniform each day. Then, of course, there was the beauty shop, the barber shop, and a small store for many needed everyday items and also an infirmary with a doctor, a druggist with his drugs, a nurse, three beds, and an examination table.

One huge pantry served the needs of all on board. Huge wire baskets on racks held tons of canned goods, and fruits and vegetables were in wooden crates along the walls. The huge walk-in freezer held beef, pork, lamb, yes, even deer carcasses on several tracks, and there were bins of turkey, poultry, pheasant, and ducks, all secured against movement should a storm come up. Butcher equipment was just outside of this cool pantry, and it required two butchers to keep up. There was a wide side door about twenty feet above the water line on the starboard side, and this would be opened while in port, and the pantry refueled. Because of the insect problem, some ports would not allow certain fruits and vegetables to enter, like Philippine bananas were not allowed in Hong Kong, but were O.K. at Shanghai. Therefore, if we had any forbidden stock on hand, the pantry men would simply toss it into their garbage disposal unit before we docked.

Flowers costing literally thousands of dollars were carried aboard mainly by well-wishers and left by our departing passengers.

We would barely leave dock before the houseboys were seen carrying these from the rooms. "Please put these in a cool place and keep them watered," was the instruction. Ninety-nine point nine per cent of these were never called for, and one hundred per cent were finally dumped at sea---regulations, you know.

For power, the ship had huge boilers fed with heavy oil, this produced steam, which spun generators, which fed electric motors, which turned a huge propeller shaft, which rotated our large propeller, which screwed us through the water. Overseeing all the intricate machinery was a core of engineers, electricians, mechanics, and grease monkeys with their own quarters one deck below waterline. They had their own dining room, which was supplied by a dumb waiter from the main kitchen.

The foredeck of our ship was full of different kinds of equipment used to dock our load or offload the cargo. This huge winch which I am standing by was used by wrapping a three inch thick hawser rope three times around. Then three or four sailors would grab the free end and by pulling hard, while the drum was turning, the friction would pull on the hawser and snug the boat against the dock.

Second Age

We are all from the Stewards' Department just relaxing on a sunny day.

The captain, first mate, doctor, and purser, together with the lesser braided brass, lived on the top deck, most in separate cabins, and shared their meals in an officers' mess hall.

Each cabin had a bell button, and when pressed, would light a small globe on our board over the cabin's number. We would then race up or down the companion way to answer the light. We would never know until we got there what they wanted, so there was always some anticipation. Most of the time it was to carry a message to another room, chase after aspirin, go after a new menu for the day or bring a double one from the bar. But there were many others.

A newly married bride, Mrs. Reynolds of the R.J. Reynolds Tobacco Company, had a huge trunk with nothing but shoes in it. When she rang and we appeared at the door, she was half dressed. I think she liked to be looked at, no matter by whom. "Please bring up my trunk with the shoes," she said. This involved going to the Purser's Office, signing out the key, waiting for the freight elevator, descending into the bowels of the ship, finding the trunk in a mountain of baggage, putting it on a two wheel roller, re-locking the room, going back by elevator, delivering it to the room, returning the key, and getting a release slip. Thirty minutes later the light came on: "I have what I need. Please remove the trunk." This happened at least twice a week. She did leave a one hundred dollar tip, however, for the bellboys, the largest we ever did get.

Another incident: a snappy, good looking woman around thirty years old had boarded at Honolulu, headed for San Francisco, and was in her cabin on the main deck. We wondered at the time why she hadn't been snapped up by certain wolves on board. I answered her bell next morning to find her sitting up in bed with very scanty attire. "Please close the door," she said. "I cannot," I said. "It is strictly against our orders." "I cannot stay in this room alone," she said. "I have a recipe for that," I said. "Really," she said. "A knock will come at your door, and a person will ask to check your passport. If you like what you see, say yes," I said, as I left to deliver a message to a certain person. She did leave a nice tip.

Another lady, with a twelve year-old daughter, was sailing to Manila to join her husband, who was an employee of Standard Oil and was stationed at Bagio, high in the mountains on the island of Luzon, where he also served as superintendent of a gold mine. She had trouble walking, so Tommy or I would take her around the Promenade in a wheel chair, while the lively daughter danced along with us. Sometimes we would just park her in a deck chair and then take the girl by her hand all over the ship. She (the mother) was a very nice person and as we neared Manila, she asked if Tommy and I would like to fly up to Bagio in the company plane, stay four hours, and then return.

The next day the four of us landed on a small field, and met the husband, who assigned a man to show us around this tiny town nestled in the jungle. This was an old mine, dug deeper and deeper till the heat was so high, the men had to work in water spray and then only two hours at time. The mine workers were all native Igarottes, not over four feet high, but wide of shoulder, deep in the chest, and legs the size of a telephone post. We were informed they were strong indeed. After a nice lunch, we said our good-byes and flew back to our ship. Yes, she left a nice tip for our group, but also a personal one for Tommy and me.

Then there was Gene Tunney (the man who defeated Jack Dempsey by retreating until Jack's old legs failed) and his new wife. They kept to themselves, spent much time reading books, and had a table for two only in the dining room. One early morning a passenger complained that the door to the exercise room was locked. I was on my way to breakfast but checked, secured a key, opened the door, and there was Gene exercising. He said he had to exercise alone and ordered me out and the door re-locked. I reported this to the head steward and went for my breakfast. Later in the day we learned that the first mate and two other caps with braid had come, knocked on the door, had it opened and told Gene he would leave that door unlocked, or they would clap him in irons and toss him in the hoosegow. There was no more trouble from him.

There was a steward for the port side deck and one for starboard, and they would serve the coffee and pastry for early risers, set out deck chairs, serve fruit juice at ten a.m., and in general see to the comfort of passengers. At happy hour they became assistant barkeepers or cocktail waiters. At dinner they became wine stewards.

But every day things would be different. For instance, the captain would host a big party and would use a deck steward now as a bartender at his own bar in his quarters, and now short a wine steward, one of us bellboys would slip the ring of keys---the symbol of a wine steward---on our neck and do our best.

The life of a bellboy was sure varied and was made more so by the spirit of cooperation among all of us. We did not abide one hundred per cent by working Union rules because we dived in and took over others' work, but we got the job done.

But not quite. Two sailors had gotten drunk aboard ship and made asses of themselves. They were put to polishing silverware in a large wooden tub filled with suds as punishment. This demeaning job for a crusty faced sailor, who had faced awesome waves and storms and scrubbed down miles of wooden planking, was a bit too much. They would watch for an opportunity, then grab a handful of silverware and quickly toss it out the open porthole. This was not silver-plated, this was real silverware that was going into the waves. In a few days we would reach San Francisco, and they would have an application in for work.

Second Age

Last Voyages on the President Coolidge

I signed on for another trip when we reached San Francisco, then traveled to visit Mrs. Maier and my sisters, and got all the news up to date. I had many things to tell them. I also displayed a pure silk shirt I had tailored for me in Hong Kong, with my initials on the pocket. Veryne gave me money and dimensions for three shirts she wanted for her husband Russ.

I had picked up the two camphor chests I had ordered at Kowloon when we came there on our return trip. These had been squeezed under my bunk, but I had figured a bit large so rode home on a very hard mattress. I had gone to the shop early, and the chests were ready and wrapped in raffia for shipping. Ropes were put around them and a carrying pole tied in, then four boys, two for each chest, carried them, following me into the ship. A Chinese security officer from the ship, who could speak English, kindly followed us and was interpreter, I paid each one twenty-five cents and gave them a bag of cull apples and oranges from the pantry. The officer then said, "I'll take them to the Chinese quarters so they can eat their fill, because it will all be taken away from them when they return to the shop." Those two chests I shipped to my brother and sister in Minneapolis.

Our second arrival in Honolulu at sunrise was like the first, and again I stood with the goose pimples.

The third day out of Honolulu toward Yokohama, a terrific storm came at us from the Aleutian Islands near Alaska. Captain Ahern said it was the worst he had ever been in. Forward movement was reduced by one half, and in thirty-six hours we drifted twenty-three knots south but not a single one forward. Many of the crew and most of the passengers were seasick.

I was en route to breakfast one morning while traveling from Shanghai to Hong Kong, when I noticed a rather tall man going through a set of physical exercises that looked different. He would fight the right side of his body with the left, so to speak, for instance, placing his hands together and pushing, first in the front and then in back, twisting his body to the right, then fight it back with the left. It was "Yin versus Yang".

The next morning it was lighter, and I could see he was walking like a thoroughbred horse about to race. His skin was tight about his face, and with his piercing almond eyes, seemed to exude power. In fact, I don't think I have ever felt a personality so strong. After we left Hong Kong where he had left the ship, we learned that he was Chiang Kai-Shek, Leader of Taiwan, traveling incognito.

During slow afternoons Tommy and I would sometimes go to the rear of the second class section, where a Chinese gaming room was usually going full swing (Chinese love to gamble). We got to playing Fan-Tan, a Chinese game where there was a rectangle printed on a cover. The sides were marked one-two-three-four. You could bet on the number or the corner to cover two numbers. We thought if he bet two corners and I the other two that one of us would always win. The operator would reach into a bucket of buttons and put a handful on the table, then a player would take a metal bell with a handle and rake under as many buttons as he wanted. All surplus buttons were removed. The bell was now lifted, and the operator, with a long, curved bamboo stick, would carefully count four buttons at a time from these buttons, and when he reached the last count, he would have either one, two, three, or four. We had visited this table and had gained about twenty dollars. We had also practiced at our station. Yes, we had a sure thing. However, by the time we reached Hong Kong, we had not one penny left, including the money advanced by Veryne for Russ' three silk shirts. One afternoon cleaned us out. The moral is: don't try to beat a man at his own game.

We were traveling south into the tropics from Hong Kong, and people had gathered into the dining room where dinner was just beginning. The door leading to the companionway opened and a man from the engineers' department two decks down hurriedly waved to Tommy and told him something.

Tommy immediately walked to the Captain's table and whispered to him, and he in turn motioned to the doctor, who followed Tommy back past our station and told me, "You come too." All four of us hurried down the steps and there in the shower room, on the floor, lay a man, completely naked, with several stab wounds, gurgling out blood. He was unconscious but alive. He needed to be brought to the infirmary at once. Tommy and I slipped one arm under each of his shoulders and carried one arm, another man carried his legs, while the doctor held his head and walked backward. In this manner we carried him to the freight elevator and went up four decks. But just as we left the elevator, the victim gave a very small shudder and was gone. The doctor with sadness and a hopeless look in his eyes just turned and walked away, leaving us to carry a corpse, head swinging, the rest of the way. Others now took over, and we went to our own quarters and changed our bloody uniforms.

We learned two men had been taking a shower in this large room equipped with six shower heads. The victim had been soaping down when by accident, the soap had shot out of his hand and hit the murderer in the face, which caused him to dash to his clothes, pull a knife and stab his fellow worker to death. He was promptly arrested by the chief mate and two officers, put into leg and arm shackles, and put into a room in the prow of the ship, where the heavy iron anchor chain was piled.

The purser, who was chief legal officer, conducted the investigation. We filled out documents, wrote our own account of what we did and saw, and by next noon appeared as called by the captain. At this meeting all evidence was presented and reviewed. Conclusions were reached. A full report was prepared, and we all signed it the following day. Before adjourning, we also were required to go to the brief funeral ceremony and watched while the body was committed to the sea. When we reached Manila a few days later, a small detachment of Philippino police arrived and conducted the prisoner, still in chains, to an Iberian ship which was in port. They would return him to Sicily, his native country. If the log of the good ship President Coolidge is still intact, my report will be in it.

Our week in Manila was again going to give us trouble. We had watched the cock fights going on daily, the squat women smoking their fat cigars while changing diapers, the poor chickens hanging alive upside down, the thin tough little ponies, pulling two-wheeled taxis, the daily funeral processions as they carried the small coffins (high infant mortality), and the painted-up male homosexuals near the theater section of town. Red, Tommy and I decided to hire a motor car and a driver who could speak English to take us out to the rural areas, the jungle and the tiny villages.

A quite old and quite battered touring car arrived, and we were off, with Tommy in the front seat and I and Red in the back. We were probably out to the edge of town when we slowed down and then stopped at a street corner. There were three men standing there, and they immediately piled in on top of us, and were trying to push us down and subdue us. Red's arm slid down below the back seat, and when it came up it held a tire iron. He was able to reach around his opponent and bring it down on the head of the man on the front seat, who was battling with Tommy, who then kicked him out. The driver now left the car next, running as fast as he could. Tommy was able to reach and take the tire iron from Red, and he now whacked the man on top of me, and I pushed him unconscious to the dirt. The last man on Red decided this was not for him and ran off. Red yelled, "Let's get out of here," and Tommy jumped into the driver's seat and we took off, leaving two still forms on the ground. We soon ran into a dead end, and when we turned around and retraced our tracks, the two men had disappeared. We found our way back into town, parked the car uptown and returned to the ship. We were to leave the next day so stayed close to our quarters, being a bit uneasy about our fight and not reporting it.

On my third trip, Manuel Quézon, President of the Philippines, and his retinue of some thirty people, boarded and occupied the best cabins. Believe me, they wanted everything done for them, and it was done. These were our orders. We peons could talk among ourselves, however, and we wondered how a man who would not even comb his own hair could govern so many islands, or how the man who did comb the President's hair could act like the King of Siam when around us.

He was eventually delivered to Manila to a great welcome home celebration. His secretary left a letter telling us that if anyone of us got into trouble, they would help us. Quite a tip at that, wasn't it?

Andy Gump was not with us this trip, nor was Red, who had transferred to another Dollar Line ship that traveled around the world.

It would be my last trip also.

On our return trip, I had made the decision to do something else, and on pondering and thinking what I should do next, I decided that it was time to move to the third stage of my life, that of service. It was time that I should begin paying back those things given to me by my parents, the good roads, schools, freedoms, everything that society had provided for me. It was time that I find my life's work, marriage, children, a home, and become a worthwhile member of my country. Having made this decision, I could barely wait to be returned to San Francisco and engage in my new life to be.

Reflecting now on the events that happened some sixty years ago and in writing these lines, it seems that I was lucky so many, many times, and I would be lucky, too, in my life of service. But all these lucky things put together would not be equal to my luck in finding and marrying Rosemary Sleeper. Together we would pass through the entire third period of service, and now hearts and hands entwined, we live a happy Golden Age.

A Little About People and Times

The President Coolidge ship: It plied the waters of the Pacific on its usual route until our war with Japan. Then it would be converted to a cargo and troop carrier. It was loaded with one hundred twenty International TD-18 crawler tractors with bulldozers and winches. As a civilian, I prepared a list of parts, ordered them, and helped a Marine Store Master receive, check in, and bin almost a million dollars' worth. The ship sailed from the Marine base at Oakland to an atoll somewhere in the South Pacific and there hit one of our own mines four miles off shore, and sank.

The floating house: Clarence and Virginia lived in it for a few years on the river. He then lengthened it and added a paddle wheel to the rear, and a wood-fired steam boiler to turn this wheel. He pushed it back up the Mississippi to the mouth of the St. Croix River and anchored it at Stillwater, Minnesota, then moved it to a bluff on the Wisconsin side.

As you will remember, I left them newly married on the floating house, tied up at a river inlet on Pettibone Island near La Crosse, Wisconsin. We sent letters back and forth for a few years, but as we both entered our lives of service, we more or less lost track of each other. Upon my retirement we motored back to Minnesota and discovered that Clarence and Virginia had moved to Salmon Creek near Bodega Bay in California, only ninety miles from our retirement ranch in Lake

County. Our motor trip return was through Texas and finally up Highway 101 in California, so we drove to Salmon Creek and while hunting for his house, we spied him coming from the post office with a package, which proved to be his proof sheets from the publisher of his one book of prose. Well, we sure did have one heck of a good visit.

He was living with his youngest daughter, who subsequently married, leaving him alone. He loved solitude. Virginia was in a rest home in Petaluma about thirty miles away, and when we visited her, though she was quite ill, she still had that sunny Irish disposition and sweet smile.

Clarence informed us that they had lived on the St. Croix River for a short time after moving the floating house to Stillwater, where he had purchased thirty-five acres of wooded land on the Wisconsin bluffs. Here he was lucky in two ways: first, there were many more logs than he figured, and the price was good. Then, they discovered high quality flagstone rock which they quarried, and built a big house around a large tree. They also shipped many tons of flagstone to the building trades.

All of the time they were doing these things they were also raising a family, and by the time they finished that project, they had nine sons and three daughters. I'm sure all of them received a full measure of love from their parents.

The writing of poetry, however, was Clarence's lifelong drive and ambition. Before his life would come to an end, he would publish six books of verse, one of prose (non-fiction), and four children's books, plus many sonnets and other writings not published.

It was now time for him to put all of life's things together and with a tired, failing and non-fixable heart, he found a friend to help put together a final group of poems, some new and some old. One of his new poems was directions for the burial of his body. I quote:

Second Age

When I have stiffened properly and well,
Lay me in a plain box in my old clothes,
No need to dress where I go now, for those
Below have neither heart to know or tell
How I come down the Dark Eternal Stairs...

I join a common crowd where vanity
Can crowd or crow no more, nor shut eyes see
What neighbor comes, or how, or what he wears.

Let Dave or Marshall haul me slowly here.
A truck will do, I do not wish a hearse.
Some corner in Bodega's simple plot-
And bring for friends an extra case of beer.
Then from old Khayyam read a simple verse,
And later raise a stone to mark the plot.

Clarence Jonk

One day, maybe six months later, Carl, their oldest son, called and said Clarence had passed on peacefully at eighty-one years. The funeral would be family only, and he would call back. Eight of the nine sons came. Together they built a plain pine box. The man who had delivered wood to Clarence with a flatbed truck now loaned it for a hearse. Two sons drove, while seven sat with the box, and all nine slowly rode the three miles to Bodega Bay, where they personally dug the hole. Yes, they brought a book of Omar Khayyam's verses, the Rubaiyat, and one was read while they were in a group around the grave. It was then covered and the case of beer opened. A stone was agreed upon and would be placed later.

I write all this because we shared an important part of our lives with each other, and the memories linger on.

As you will recall, I had mentioned that I was now ready to enter the Third Age of my life---that of service. During the time of my return trip from the Philippine Islands, I dreamed and plotted and planned how to accomplish this.

First I would find any kind of a job to sustain myself and at the same time locate work in a field that would lead me to happiness and contentment during my service life. Second I was now a mature drake (farm talk) and it was time that I chose a young goose from the gaggle of geese and be mated for life for that was the way of my Viking forefathers and the way I was taught.

In more or less rapid succession, I had my nose operated on for sinus problems while I could receive it free from my maritime union. I sold silk hosiery for five months, made beans and bacon, and received good intensive sales training. But it was not for me. Then I sold household refrigerators, got in an argument over earnings, and quit. I joined a popular club (five thousand strong in San Francisco), was disillusioned and with others dropped out. I took a Dale Carnegie course in self-improvement which was extremely rewarding to me.

The Oakland to San Francisco Bay Bridge was being built. A friend gave me a tip about a night watchman job and I was hired when I applied. Traveling to work, I boarded the ferry at the dock in San Francisco, crossed the bay to the Oakland slip, then walked through a door on the west side of the dock. From there I crossed over the bay on a short, floating foot bridge to the base of the first bridge footing. Then I climbed a long, somewhat shaky, zig-zag stairway to the floor of the

Second Age

bridge. From here it was a short walk forward to the edge of the construction where there was a small portable shack with lights, heat, desk and a phone.

The bridge from San Francisco to Yerba Buena Island was of cable suspension construction. The other from this island to Oakland was of cantilever design and as work progressed, the shack was moved forward, sometimes hanging out over the bay with only a few planks and steel beams beneath. It was then when the storms raged and the shack was shaken that I became a bit scared.

There was absolutely nothing to do there. I think I answered the phone twice, called in once when a sheet of plywood blew loose and sailed off into the darkness, and turned back two boys who had slipped onto the bridge on a moonlit night.

The shack was warm, with a good light, chair and desk so I wrote a lot of past due letters, read some good books, and even composed a couple of the world's worst poems. Then, too, I planned and planned for the future and daydreamed of the day I could ask my future wife to be mine.

Somehow I arrived at the conclusion that I must return to some phase of agriculture. I was of the soil---born and raised on a farm. I had all of my college training in agronomy and plant pathology and now longed to return to the people I knew, trusted and felt at home with.

My future wife had many relatives. One of them was in the management team for International Harvester Co. and soon I was working for them in the parts department during the day. I had a full-time night job as well as the daytime one but still pursued my courtship full steam ahead.

Thus, without fanfare, my Second Age passed into the Third.

Second Age

Index

Accordion   48, 63, 65, 85, 86, 90, 126
Anoka   90

Barge(s)   26, 30, 31, 32, 35
Bagio   129
Barrels   41, 42, 47, 50, 56, 64, 68, 122
Buttermilk   28, 31, 37, 39, 43, 51, 61, 66, 122

China   99, 110
Chippewa Indians   46, 77
               River   44
Clarence (Jonk)   29, 30, 32, 34, 35, 37, 39, 40, 41, 47, 48, 52, 53, 55, 57, 58, 63, 68, 83, 84, 85, 93, 122, 138, 139, 140
Como Avenue   22
Corn shocks   33
Creamery   28, 31, 39, 61
Cribbing   20, 21, 23

Dairy   37, 72, 83, 121
Daley   60, 62, 62, 64, 65, 67, 68, 71, 76, 77, 78, 79, 80, 82, 84, 85
Diamond Bluff   34
Dollar (Steamship) Lines   98, 121
Dollies   21, 23
Dresbach Dam   76

Farallone Islands   95, 100
Fisherman's Wharf   92
Five-gallon milk cans   28
Floating house   24, 25

Hastings   32, 33
Hong Kong   132, 133, 134
Honolulu   102, 104, 129, 132, 133

Inland Sea   110

Jack (dog)   30, 32, 33, 34, 35, 36, 37, 38, 39, 42, 43, 44, 47, 50, 54, 55, 56, 58, 65, 69, 71, 83, 101
Japan   99, 104, 105, 106, 110, 111, 125, 138
Junk (boat)   110

Kobe   105
Kowloon   116, 117, 119, 132

La Crescent   60, 62, 66, 75, 79, 80
La Crosse   75, 76, 80, 85
Lake City   42, 45

Index

Lake Johanna   13
Lake Pepin   40, 41, 44, 47
Linchpin   22

Manila   rope, 52
         city, 99, 113, 120, 121, 122, 124, 129, 135, 136
Meekers Island   27
Minneapolis   27, 46, 85, 90, 117, 121, 132
Minnehaha Creek   27
Minnesota Island   54, 71
Mississippi   31, 41, 42, 44, 51, 57, 70, 71, 80, 138
Mr. Harris   22, 23
Mrs. Maier   91, 98, 99, 132

Pike pole   26, 27, 33, 39, 51, 52, 57, 71, 72, 73
Poodle Dog Bar   122, 123
President Coolidge   98, 99, 135, 138
Propeller   26, 32, 38, 39, 42, 43, 52, 56, 100, 102, 120, 127

Railroad tracks   54, 60, 64, 72, 73, 82
Red Wing   37, 38, 39
River ice   50
Rock wing dam   48, 53, 54

San Francisco   90, 91, 92, 93, 100, 101, 102, 104, 113, 122, 129, 131, 132,
         137, 141, 142
School of Agriculture   12, 14, 93
Shanghai   110, 111, 113, 125, 126, 133
Southern Cross   119
Stillwater   46, 138, 139
St. Croix River   32, 46, 138, 139
St. Paul 27, 28, 29, 46, 68, 84, 93

Trempealeau   46

University Avenue   20

Winona   47, 77

Yangtze or Yellow River   110
Yokohama   104, 105, 133

Second Age

About the Author

Carl Franson was one of ten children, of whom seven survived, born to hard-working, first generation immigrants. Working to make your way in life was second nature to him. He possessed a intense curiosity about life, people, and the natural wonders around him. This openness comes through in his story about his life as a young man on the Upper Mississippi, in San Francisco, and during travels to the Far East.

Second Age

www.ingramcontent.com/pod-product-compliance
Lightning Source LLC
Chambersburg PA
CBHW070810100426
42742CB00012B/2323